Dennis McIntosh is a playwright, writer and educator whose work explores the politics of labour and working-class life. After a long working life in manual and industrial labour, he returned to university aged 40, an experience he describes as 'living life twice'. His academic research has informed his creative practice, including an honours thesis on manual work, family relationships and language; a master's thesis on shearing and social realism; and a PhD examining tunnel work and representations of blue-collar labour in literature. His published works include *Beaten By a Blow* and *The Tunnel* (Penguin Books), both based on his own memories. His plays include *I Is Maggie*, about migrant women working in an industrial laundry, and *West Gate*, which examines the 1970 bridge collapse that killed 35 workers. Dennis works as a teacher and has taught in remote Indigenous communities across the Northern Territory and Queensland, and now teaches literacy in a diverse learning hub at a multicultural school.

WEST GATE

By Dennis McIntosh

CURRENCY PRESS
The performing arts publisher

MELBOURNE THEATRE COMPANY

CURRENT THEATRE SERIES

First published in 2026
by Currency Press Pty Ltd,
Gadigal Land, Suite 310, 46–56 Kippax Street, Surry Hills, NSW 2010, Australia
enquiries@currency.com.au
www.currency.com.au

in association with Melbourne Theatre Company.

Reprinted 2026.

Typeset by Brighton Gray for Currency Press.
Printed by Fineline Print and Copy Services, Revesby NSW.
Cover photograph by Jo Duck.
Cover design by Sarah Ridgway-Cross.
Front cover shows Daniela Farinacci and Steve Bastoni.

Currency Press acknowledges the Traditional Owners of the Country on which we live and work. We pay our respects to all Aboriginal and Torres Strait Islander Elders, past and present.

A catalogue record for this book is available from the National Library of Australia

Contents

Writer Dennis McIntosh and director Iain Sinclair in rehearsal. (Photo: Emily Doyle)

Ben Walter in rehearsal. (Photo: Charlie Kinross)

Author's Note

At 11:50 a.m. on 15 October 1970, I was an eleven-year-old boy standing on the netball court on top of the Sacred Heart Primary School in Newport. I was looking through the cyclone wire fence at the mighty West Gate Bridge that was being built across the horizon. It had just collapsed while under construction and the thud radiated out across the western suburbs of Melbourne. We were all touched by it in that moment, and it has forever more been burned into my consciousness. The rumours around the school and town at that time were that the bridge was going to fall. Then it did.

My father had the same initials and surname as the resident engineer on the bridge, D.F. McIntosh. As the Royal Commission on the Failure of a Portion of the West Gate Bridge will attest, D.F. McIntosh wrote several letters of concern about several aspects of the bridge procedures to his London office. What the Royal Commission does not say is that the returning correspondence often went to our house in Schutt Street, Newport. I remember Dad opening a letter and proclaiming, 'There is something wrong with the bridge'. Hence the rumours were galvanised in my mind. Over the years I wondered what really happened.

In August 2013, I began my quest to write this story and let the men who died—who had no justice—tell their story. *West Gate* is that story. During the years of writing it, I kept photos of the men who had died on top of my computer to remind me never to give up on their story.

A story of this magnitude doesn't reach production on the back of one person. I had completed my research during Covid, and in 2021 I started writing. With a script in hand, I received a small funding grant from Cairns Regional Arts Development Funding and staged a development at the Jute Theatre Company in Cairns. Australian theatre director Iain Sinclair read it as a favour to a friend and came on board. Iain is the bridge between this new work and the world of theatre. I have always felt empowered as a writer working with Iain. It is a wonderful feeling to work with someone who believes in you.

Sometimes in life, someone else has the key to the door you cannot open. In the case of *West Gate* that person is Jenni Medway, the Head of New Work at Melbourne Theatre Company, and I will always be grateful to Jenni for the opportunity she has afforded this story. It is my fervent hope that when this story is performed, those men will once more live again and get to tell their own story.

Every writer needs a Woree State High School behind them. As a teacher, I had months off at a time writing drafts, and the staff always took an interest in my work and were warm and supportive. The students are the souls of the earth. Thanks particularly to Renee Krauss, who looked after me over the last few years—thank you. I could not have completed this writing project without your support.

Finally, to my wife, Maggie, who threatens to divorce me if I write another story. Thank you. At this stage I'm hanging in there with her.

Dr Dennis McIntosh

A SPECIAL NOTE OF THANKS

I would especially like to thank Danny Gardiner from the Westgate bridge memorial committee for his help and support in contacting survivors and children of victims of the disaster. Danny also supported me in the process of writing the play.

Thank you to Tommy Watson who I interviewed in 2013 and was always generous with his time. Victor Geruda was 3-month-old when his father was killed. Victor provided invaluable insights into life for himself, his siblings and his mother in the years following the death of their father.

Pat Preston who was on the ground as a crane driver when the bridge fell. Pat was always available for questions and explanations to get a first-hand account of the day and life afterwards for the men. Finally, Vinny Roseworne who is the last survivor of the 18 men who rode the bridge down and lived. Vinny has been a constant supporter of this project and of me. Vinny has attended Creative Developments and shared his first-hand experiences of the day and the years afterwards living with the disabilities and physical scars left by the disaster.

Darcy Kent in rehearsals. (Photo: Charlie Kinross)

Paul English, Peter Houghton and Darcy Kent in rehearsals. (Photo: Charlie Kinross)

Stephen Maiden, Rohan Nichol and Darcy Kent in rehearsals. (Photo: Charlie Kinross)

Steve Bastoni and Daniela Farinacci in rehearsals. (Photo: Charlie Kinross)

West Gate was first produced by the Melbourne Theatre Company at Southbank Theatre, The Sumner, Melbourne, on the lands of the Boon Wurrung and Wurundjeri Woi Wurrung peoples of the Kulin Nation, on 10 March 2026 with the following cast and creatives:

VICTOR	Steve Bastoni
STEVENSON	Paul English
FRANKIE	Daniela Farinacci
McALISTER	Peter Houghton
YOUNG SCRAPPER	Darcy Kent
VINNY	Simon Maiden
PAT	Rohan Nichol
COOPER	Ben Walter

Director, Iain Sinclair
Set & Costume Designer, Christina Smith
Assistant Set & Costume Designer, Bianca Pardo
Lighting Designer, Niklas Pajanti
Composer & Sound Designer, Kelly Ryall
Voice & Dialect Coach, Anna McCrossin-Owen
Dramaturg, Iain Sinclair
Assistant Set and Costume Designer, Bianca Pardo
Assistant Director, Laura Ozzimo
Stage Manager, Juliette Hirons
Deputy Stage Manager, Annah Jacobs
Assistant Stage Manager, Rain Iyahen

Melbourne Theatre Company acknowledges the Boon Wurrung and Wurundjeri Woi Wurrung peoples of the Kulin Nation, the Traditional Custodians of the land on which we work, create and gather. We pay our respects to all First Nations people, their Elders past and present, and their enduring connections to Country, knowledge, and stories. As a Company we remain committed to the invitation of the Uluru Statement from the Heart and its call for voice, truth and treaty.

NEXTSTAGE

Developed through Melbourne Theatre Company's NEXT STAGE Writers' Program, with the support of our Playwrights Giving Circle.

CHARACTERS

FRANKIE (Francesca, Italian): wife of Victor

Workers

VICTOR: Welder, Italian migrant. Also known as Vittorio.

YOUNG SCRAPPER: Labourer, young English immigrant. He is the son of a well-known pub fighter regarded as the toughest scrapper in the construction industry.

PAT: Crane driver/shop steward. Aussie.

B.J. (BARRY JONES): Derrick driver and toppy, Australian-born, gambler.

Engineers

MCALISTER: Resident Engineer, brought in by Rathbone and Watt.

STEVENSON: Consulting with Masons and Sons, London branch. Liaises with Westgate Bridge Authority and in charge of contracts.

COOPER: Young contract engineer for the Drilling and Concrete Construction Company. Has been moved onto the job to get it finished.

NOTE

'Westgate' refers to the Westgate Bridge.

'West Gate' refers to the gate entry on the western side of the construction site.

This playtext went to press before the end of rehearsals and may differ from the play as performed.

ACT ONE

SCENE ONE

7 a.m., 12 June 1970. Westgate Bridge construction site.

The curtain rises with a half-built Westgate Bridge. There are industrial sounds and sights such as hammering, motors running, welding sparks and cranes. Reversing lights flashing and warning beeps. The bridge is swaying. The wind is howling. One by one the sounds disappear until we have silence.

B.J. *blows his whistle.*

Silence.

B.J.: Under below.

Union meeting, 8 a.m. 12 June 1970.

PAT: Okay lads, settle down, settle down. Ooohhh, come to order.

Heavy chatter.

YOUNG SCRAPPER: Can we go home after the meetin'?

Jeers and laughs.

PAT: It's already eight o'clock in the morning, comrades. Markillies'll be shutting soon.

Jeers.

Okay, okay, quieten down. Now most've you know why we're here.

YOUNG SCRAPPER: Cos the bridge is gonna fall down.

B.J.: Who let him back.

He shakes his head.

YOUNG SCRAPPER: Watch out or my old man'll give you anovver floggin'.

He laughs.

B.J.: Not from Pentridge he won't.

All laugh.

PAT: Fuck me. Can we start this meeting without starting World War Three? Young Scrapper, zip it.

B.J.: Have you checked if all the west side boys are here yet?

PAT *stares at* B.J.

PAT: Do you want to stand up so everyone can see you?

B.J.: [*under his breath*] Smartarse.

PAT: Ay, listen up. Put your hand up if you're here. And no ghosting. If someone's not here I need to know. Know you're here, Young Scrapper, Bigmore, Barbuto, Boscolo, Carmichael, Dawson, Eden, Falzon, Fernandez, Fitzsimmonds—

Looks.

Lads, put your hands up so I can see 'em. Grist, Gerada, Harburn, Hunsdale, Little, Lund, McGuire, Murphy, O'Brien— [*Yelling*] O'Brien. Do you want a personal fucken invitation to put your hand up? Well put ya fucken hand up. Ozelis, Piermarini, Pram, Scarlett, Stewart, Suarez, Tsihilidis, Upsdell, Whelan, Woods, Wright, Westie is your boy ready to play for the Doggies? Good on ya mate.

Victor you here? Okay I see you now. We good.

Now we all need to work and we wanna work. And we wanna make it home at the end a the day. That's all. Just to recap. In Wales ten days ago a bridge in the Welsh town of Milford Haven collapsed. The bridge was a Rathbone and Watt design. Same mob that's buildin' this bridge. And it was a box girder bridge like our bridge. So.

One, we want to know that our job hasn't got the same problems as the Milford Haven Bridge.

MEN *low approval; cheers.*

Two, we wanna know that the engineers have got this bridge—our fucken bridge—under control.

Cheering louder.

Three, we wanna know that we will get home tonight … and every other night.

Cheers loudest.

Okay, you would've seen Mr Stevenson from Masons and Sons around the traps. He's been here from the beginning. Alongside him is Mr Cooper. His crew did all the drilling and built the pilings, did most of the concreting, and as you would have seen they've taken over erecting the rest of the box girders on the west side. Finally we have Mr McAlister from the design team Rathbone and Watt, and no, he's not the Lord Mayor of fucken London either. But he is, so to speak, fresh off the boat. He is McIntosh's replacement as the resident engineer on the west side.

WORKERS: Where's McIntosh? / What happened to him?

STEVENSON *steps forward.*

STEVENSON: If I may Pat. McIntosh has been out here in Australia for a number of years and I know that his family wanted him back at home.

Looks at PAT.

PAT: Well he made it known some of the steel coming onsite was buckled? Did he complain too much? That's what I'm asking.

MEN *rumble.*

B.J.: Actually, his whinging was more specifically about having no guidelines to measure the straightness tolerances of the steel sheets.

PAT *stares at him for stealing his thunder, then throws his hands up.*

PAT: [*to* B.J.] Didn't I just say that?

STEVENSON: Gentlemen, he was reassigned. That's all. Mr McAlister has been specifically brought over from London because of his expertise.

PAT: Okay well, let's hear what he's got to say. Listen up.

MCALISTER: Thank you Pat. Men, I am the new engineer in charge of the west side. You would have seen me walking around the site over the last few weeks. It's understandable you have concerns about our bridge, and it is true the Milford Haven Bridge that partially collapsed in Wales recently was one of ours. It would spook me too, if I thought this bridge was the same as that one. But I can assure you men our bridge, the mighty Westgate Bridge will not fall down.

YOUNG SCRAPPER: How do we know that?

ALL WORKERS: Shut up.

MCALISTER: Well, that's what I'm hear to tell you. This bridge has been designed by Mr Rathbone and Sir John Bancroft himself, and they are regarded as the greatest bridge designers in the modern world. Hell, they even built the Sydney Harbour Bridge and that came out alright, didn't it? However, just as a precaution, we have commissioned a report on the Milford Haven Bridge and we will find out what went wrong. And if there are any similarities to this bridge, we'll fix them.

B.J.: It's our lives on the line up there, mate. We're the ones actually doing the work.

MCALISTER: And what's your name?

PAT *and other* MEN *react to* B.J. *putting himself forward.*

B.J.: Vinny, Vinny / Rose.

YOUNG SCRAPPER: —We call him Barry fucken Jones cos he thinks he knows everythin'.

MCALISTER: —Well B.J., that's true.

All laugh. MCALISTER *has a win.*

You are the ones up in the air doing the work, I grant you that, and you are doing a mighty job up there too. But I'll tell you why you should go back to work and not worry. Because I am the best bridge builder from here to India and I've built half the fooken bridges round the world. I know what I'm doing, lads. And I'll be on the bridge with you every step of the way. My old man was a quarryman, lads. He wouldn't take to me being a coffee-sucking desk jockey. I'm a feet-on-the-ground engineer. I'll be with you every step of the way.

Men, look how far you've come. Sure we've had delays and setbacks, but it's in the skyline, boys, and it's the biggest bridge of its kind in the world. And you're building it. You have my word on its safety. Now let's finish this fooken bridge, lads.

PAT: Okay. Thanks Mr McAlister. You blokes will have to leave now and the men'll discuss it.

Turns back to the MEN.

Now we're going to do this properly. I need a motion and I need a seconder to that motion. Then we'll have one person speak for the motion, *fucken one.* And then we'll have one person speak against the motion. Then we'll vote. That's it. Now where's that

Irishman Murphy? You: don't bring up the Altona Main Roads cockup. And for that matter, Bullshit, where are you? No talk on the Port Melbourne garbage dispute, either. Got it? Right, one more—Shakespeare, put your hand up.

Finds him in the crowd, locks eyes and points.

No long-winded personal stories, is that clear? Rightio Victor, you've had your hand up long enough. You got the floor.

VICTOR: Thanks Pat. You know I not born here. My old man, he came from Italy after the war. But this is our home. We don't have nowhere else. And it is a good country.

YOUNG SCRAPPER: Stop the wog from waffling, Pat, and get to the point.

WORKERS: Hey, keep ya trap shut boy, you can't speak like that—

VICTOR: —Okay, okay. It's okay. [*To* YOUNG SCRAPPER] You Aboriginal? No. If I'm wog, you're wog too. So we're all wogs. I have union ticket, I'm a member, see. So I can speak and I'm Australian and I have ticket for that too.

PAT: Come on Victor. Don't turn it into a citizenship ceremony. Get to the point, and you, Young Scrapper, shut up.

VICTOR: My wife, Frankie, she wants me to take her for a drive over the bridge one day. She say, get me out of bloody Altona for a day. She want to see how the other side live.

MEN *laugh.*

And I want to tell my children one day when we drive over it, 'hey, I work on that bridge'.

But we all hear the bolt snap and the steel scream sometime. We see the rust lift off the sheets. Shhheesh. And every week they change their bloody mind.

I do worry, for sure I do. But if the engineer say he gonna be on the bridge with us, it must be safe. They have to know what they are doing. So I say we go back to work. Anyway they can't kill all of us.

YOUNG SCRAPPER: They'd love to but.

PAT: Settle down. Thanks Victor. So Victor's motion is to continue on the job while we wait for the report on our bridge's safety. Is that right, Victor?

VICTOR: Good enough Pat.

PAT: Okay do I have a seconder?

Looks around.

Thanks Bullshit. We have a seconder to Victor's motion. Okay B.J. you got the floor.

MEN *laugh.*

B.J. *puts two fingers up.*

B.J.: You would do well to listen, then. Look, this job is riddled with mistakes. Look at the buckled sheets they had to fix on the east side. But we did fix them. Anyway we can't keep crossing over on the punt, and Dynan Road's chockers in the morning. We need this bridge. And it's long-term steady work—

Stares at PAT.

—when we're not on strike for piddly-arsed things.

PAT *stares at* B.J. *Shakes his head.*

But under these circumstances, where our safety is in question, we need to stop work until we know this bridge is safe—

YOUNG SCRAPPER: —Look, this job's had more fuck-ups than a whorehouse on pay day.

PAT: Are you seconding the motion?

YOUNG SCRAPPER: Yeah. Looks like it, don't it. And don't you wogs go voting to go back ta work just so you can buy anovver house and bring anovver load of your family out 'ere neiver.

WORKERS: Get him outta here. Can you shut him up?

PAT: Rightio. The first motion by Victor is to return to work and wait to see the engineer's report. All in favour raise your hands.

PAT *counts.*

Mmmm, okay, the fors have it. It's back to work, fellas, and no recriminations. We got enough going wrong without a war against each other.

YOUNG SCRAPPER: Okay Pat, I'm pullin' the pin. Good luck gettin' anywhere with some of these scabby bastards.

PAT: You're not goin' anywhere. You just got put back on yerself. So stop your carry-on. And there's no-one more safety-conscious than Victor. So don't try any shenanigans with him, got it?

And while I'm at it, most of our crew weren't born here. You included. So get off his back. Go on, piss off and get to work.

B.J. *shakes his head.*

SCENE TWO

8 a.m., 2 July 1970. Box girder.

VICTOR *is welding K-plates when* YOUNG SCRAPPER *comes in. He has a welding shield, a handheld welder from a portable welder with flux rods. Welding fumes fill the air and he uses a heavy hammer.* YOUNG SCRAPPER *picks up a welding shield and watches the welding.*

YOUNG SCRAPPER: Hey, that's beautiful welding there. You're weaving that molten steel like a maestro, mate. And the steel's movin' and the bridge is swayin' and you haven't missed a single weave. Ya gonna be in the weldin' hall a fame one day. Nearly as good as me old man. And that's sayin somethin'.

VICTOR *takes off shield and holds up a K-plate.*

VICTOR: Shit. Look, they too thin, too small. They weak.

YOUNG SCRAPPER: Fuck, it's you. Didn't know wogs could weld.

VICTOR: Now you know wogs can weld, boy.

YOUNG SCRAPPER: Hey, you can't call me boy. I look young cos I'm handsome, that's all. And I'm on full pay too, mate. Full fucken pay.

VICTOR: [*muttering to himself*] Now we change one K-plate with the same K-plate? Crazy. And look, they use a mild steel for this job. No good.

YOUNG SCRAPPER: Hello, hello, you talkin' to me? You talkin' to me? Cos I'm over 'ere if you can't see. 'Ere.

VICTOR: For young man you say a lot, and you're new on the job too. No experience.

YOUNG SCRAPPER: Well, I was on the job when it started and fucked off fer a while.

VICTOR: Ahh I see, Young the Scrap.

YOUNG SCRAPPER: See what?

VICTOR: Your missus, hey, she— [*Throwing his hand up*] got the new one.

YOUNG SCRAPPER: Fuck off, will ya? Na. I just had things to do. Anyway, they rang me up, said they couldn't build the bridge without me. So I'm back.

VICTOR: Che pezzo di merda è questo ragazzo. [What a load of shit this kid is.]

YOUNG SCRAPPER: Hey, now ya bein' rude. If ya wanna say somethin', say it to me face. And don't worry 'bout that shit ya weldin' neither. They're concretin' 'em in.

VICTOR: Who say that?

Whistle blows for smoko.

YOUNG SCRAPPER: Don't know, just heard it yesterdy. Layin' the concrete base for the road down 'ere.

YOUNG SCRAPPER *pulls out his thermos and sits on the wall.* VICTOR *sits down, takes out salami, bread and knife.* VICTOR *looks out onto the half-built bridge edging onto the skyline.*

VICTOR: That dust it burning my eyes.

YOUNG SCRAPPER: Yeah, nah, that's not dust, mate. The driver said it's ash from burnt coal. They use it to strengthen the concrete.

YOUNG SCRAPPER *picks his teeth, showing* VICTOR *where the dust gets in.*

See.

VICTOR *looks, then turns to look out across the bridge's skyline.*

VICTOR: Look, look the curve of the bridge in the sky against the bend in the river. It a big job we on. Steady work that good for our families.

YOUNG SCRAPPER: Hope they don't fuck it up.

VICTOR: Anyway, what you real name, son?

YOUNG SCRAPPER: Not ya son neither. Name's Scrapper to you. My old man was the real scrapper, could fight like a thrashing machine. When he walked into a pub everyone knew it. You didn't look my old man in the eye. He was that tough. They just called him The Scrapper. And I'm the son of The Scrapper. Young Scrapper.

VICTOR: Okay Young the Scrap, want a bit salami?

VICTOR *spits the dust out.*

YOUNG SCRAPPER: Piss off, don't eat wog food.

VICTOR: Come, try. Made it myself. Homemade salami. Good for you. Could help, huh. [*Parodying Aussie slang*] Make your cock stand right up.

YOUNG SCRAPPER: Don't need help with that, alright … Can't hurt I suppose. Oii, it's fucken hot.

VICTOR *laughs.*

VICTOR: Yes, good for you.

YOUNG SCRAPPER: I shouldn't have trusted you. Ya tryin' to kill me so ya can get them cousins of yours out 'ere to take me job.

VICTOR *laughs.*

VICTOR: That good wog food, real wog food, Young the Scrap.

YOUNG SCRAPPER: Scrapper, it's Young Scrapper.

VICTOR: Okay, well, where your lunch anyway, convict? If you not wog then have to be convict.

YOUNG SCRAPPER: We didn't come out with the First Fleet mate. We came out on a plane. I'm a fucken pom. Lived in the migrant hostel at Wiltona up the road there. I might end up a convict but. Anyway, let me eat me pie now.

VICTOR: Why eat that shit food? Get your wife to cook something.

YOUNG SCRAPPER: Mate I told ya already, don't have one. Don't want one and don't need one. They're just trouble mate.

VICTOR: My father, he wise man to say 'Senza moglie a lato, l'uomo non é beato.' Without the wife, the man is not blessed.

YOUNG SCRAPPER: Alright, alright. Don't have to bang on about it.

Drinks his tea.

VICTOR: You have tea. I have grappa. Want some? Puts hairs on your balls, mate.

YOUNG SCRAPPER: What's with all this cock and ball shit? That's fucken private, mate, ya shouldn't be talkin like that. Not out—

He looks around.

—'ere anyways.

VICTOR *laughs.*

VICTOR: You not so tough, huh. You know my wife, Francesca, everyone call her Frankie, she come over from Italia to marry me.

My family arrange the wedding. I met her on my wedding day. It's just a lucky dip mate. Just a lucky dip.

YOUNG SCRAPPER *eats his pie and drinks his tea.*

Come on, have some bread. Here, take it. Go on. And give me try of your Aussie pie.

YOUNG SCRAPPER *takes a bite.*

YOUNG SCRAPPER: Not bad, better than ya salami, mate. Did ya missus make that too?

VICTOR: No, got it at the pie shop.

He laughs.

Tell me, who this Barry Jones?

YOUNG SCRAPPER: Barry Jones? Just a geezer on a game show. He knew everything you don't need to fucken know and he won it.

VICTOR *laughs.*

VICTOR: Okay. Let's cut the rest of K-plates out before we weld in knew ones.

YOUNG SCRAPPER: 'Nother five minutes, ay. No rush, mate. This job's on the never-never.

VICTOR: What's this never-never?

YOUNG SCRAPPER: It's never, never gonna finish.

VICTOR: You not as funny as you think, huh?

YOUNG SCRAPPER: Well, I think I'm pretty funny and I think you're fucken borin'.

Stretches out.

VICTOR: That what Frankie think too. She say I'm hard-working but she mean boring. She say, after we marry, I'm not very funny either. I say, 'You want funny or faithful?' She think about it for a while. She come back and say, 'Okay, she can be funny for both of us'. Now she okay with boring.

Okay Young the Scrap, men work, boys play. C'mon little skip.

YOUNG SCRAPPER *gets up, starts work.*

YOUNG SCRAPPER: You can't tell me what to do? Told ya I'm on full pay, mate. Your not the fucken boss o' me.

VICTOR: Listen, huh. You my eyes and ears when I weld, huh? I safe because of you. That your numero uno job. You look for any danger, pick up rubbish, clean the welds but when I weld you look, you listen, huh?

VICTOR *starts welding. Stops and looks back to* YOUNG SCRAPPER. *Uses his finger to point.*

Hey. Eyes and ears.

SCENE THREE

Late July 1970. West Gate Bridge construction site.

STEVENSON *walks in and takes his hard hat off, loosens his tie, sits on desk.* MCALISTER *follows and hangs his hat on hook.*

STEVENSON: Very well accomplished I would say Mr McAlister. Yes, very good.

MCALISTER: Thank you Mr Stevenson.

STEVENSON: You have quite the—

COOPER: —The way with words—

STEVENSON: —Rhetorical skills I was thinking. The envy of the world.

MCALISTER: Confidence is earned Mr Stevenson. Confidence is earned.

COOPER: Most impressive Mr McAlister, most impressive.

MCALISTER: So where are we up to?

STEVENSON: Well, I would say, if we complete our contract—

He laughs.

—with your help of course Mr McAlister, without any delays, cost blowouts or major catastrophes, I'll be happy with that.

MCALISTER: Sounds good to me Mr Stevenson. What about this young fella? So I heard you were mainly concreters and carpenters, good ones though.

COOPER: Yes, the best in the business.

STEVENSON: And we're backing you to fix the west side. He has been working on the viaducts and the pilings on the east and the west side and he has addressed the east side problems with diligence.

MCALISTER: Well done, things are looking up for you.

COOPER: Thank you gentlemen.

STEVENSON: Now … there is one small issue I wish to broach with you. Mr Cooper's crew, they don't have much experience with steel bridges. As I said they are very good with preset concrete erections and so on but as far as steel spans go, well, they have been brought over on short notice after, as you know, World Services were sacked. And we are very appreciative of them breaching the gap. That's where you come in. It would be very very helpful if you could, as a representative of Rathbone and Watt, mentor him to some extent.

MCALISTER: Have you worked on a steel bridge before?

COOPER: This is my first time.

MCALISTER *laughs.*

MCALISTER: It's your first time, is it?

COOPER: Yes, yes.

MCALISTER: A fooken virgin, hey.

COOPER: We bring jobs in on time and on budget as Mr Stevenson said. And we will deliver on this west side as we did on the east side.

MCALISTER: I'll tell you everything I know, which is a lot.

COOPER: Thanks Mr McAlister. Well if you could drop off what stress levels we need on those boxes when we lift them that would be tremendous.

MCALISTER: I shan't be doing that.

STEVENSON: I beg your pardon?

MCALISTER: That's up to the construction engineers to work out. We're not fooken building it. We designed it.

STEVENSON: Mr McAlister we just agreed—

MCALISTER: —I'll help where I can.

STEVENSON: Pardon?

MCALISTER: I'll help him as much as I can, I said.

COOPER: With respect Mr McAlister, after the collapse of the Milford Haven Bridge I am just trying to do my due diligence so we have the correct stress levels on the boxes before we lift them into place.

MCALISTER: This bridge has nothing to do with the Milford Haven. The report will almost certainly show that the Milford Haven was fooked up because some idiot put it up wrong.

STEVENSON: Ahh.

MCALISTER: Not because of its design.

STEVENSON: I think you are jumping the gun—

MCALISTER: —I'll give you all the help I can—

COOPER: —With respect Mr McAlister …

STEVENSON: —I must remind you that the whole idea of box girders is extremely new technology.

MCALISTER: It works.

STEVENSON: Well, something went wrong at Milford Haven and until we get that report we can't second guess ourselves. We need to withhold / our judgement …

MCALISTER: Hold on / hold on—

COOPER: —Mr Stevenson, if I may, if I may. Some of our engineers don't know how the bridge is standing, they think if it ever does get finished it'll collapse under its own weight. It might be my first bridge but it doesn't take a genius to see it's so under-designed.

STEVENSON: He is saying that because of the mistakes on the east side.

MCALISTER: What happened on the east side has nothing to do with me or this job. If people don't trust each other people don't get things done. Why the Milford Haven fell down, I don't fooken know. But the report will almost certainly say it was in the execution. That sort of talk poisons a job. We are going to put that box two hundred feet in the fooken air and I know it's going to work.

COOPER: But we—

MCALISTER: —Sorry, I'll tell you why, sir. Because we've done it ten thousand times. Milford Haven is an anomaly. Box girder, not a box girder, or concrete, I don't give a fook. It didn't fall down because of our design.

COOPER: Fair enough. Then what reinforcements do you suggest we use to strengthen the failing joins? I've got K-plates pinging off left right and centre up there. With respect, sir, that's why we need those revised specs and drawings.

MCALISTER: Even you asking me that tells me you don't understand your fooken job. That's the only tangible job you have to do: reinforce that bridge. Put it to-fooken-gether. Work it out.

STEVENSON: Mr McAlister.

MCALISTER: He doesn't understand—

STEVENSON: Mr McAlister, excuse me. Sir John Bancroft himself agreed your company would supply additional calculations and camber stresses to Cooper's crew. Do you understand that?

MCALISTER: Yes I do, sir.

STEVENSON: And these drawings that you have supplied us with are only the early drafts used in the tender. They are not relevant to where the bridge is at now. The bridge has gone through several incarnations since then. They are simply not good enough. We want the updated specs and lifting calculations for live loads.

COOPER: Thank you Mr Stevenson.

MCALISTER *clears his throat.*

MCALISTER: … Look, we have given you everything you need to build the bridge. I'm here to explain how to do it. There is nothing missing. We could get new drawings and they'd say exactly what I'm saying. Consulting engineers, which is what I am, don't do this fooken job Mr Stevenson.

COOPER: [*scoffing*] So we're no better off with him here than we were before. Look, that's all well and good but when it sinks in that we have a legally bound no-fault contract you might want to reconsider this, this bluster.

MCALISTER: Why did you write one of them up?

COOPER: Why?

MCALISTER: You know what my contract is? My reputation and my word. I don't snivel around lawyers.

COOPER: See how that holds up in court.

MCALISTER: Let's see how the bridge holds up.

COOPER: What, with belief?

STEVENSON: Gentlemen.

MCALISTER: No, with good design.

STEVENSON: Gentlemen. I want—

MCALISTER: —And good execution.

STEVENSON: Gentlemen, can I—

COOPER: There's nothing wrong with my execution.

STEVENSON: Gentlemen, gentlemen. This relationship has to work. It is essential for the success of this project.

Both MCALISTER *and* COOPER *nod.*

MCALISTER: I understand, but this is no place for cowboys.

COOPER *scoffs.*

COOPER: That's a lot coming from you.

MCALISTER: Like I said in the meeting, mate. I was born on a bridge.

COOPER: Look, my men haven't missed a beat in five years. I appreciate you're new and things are done differently. You may not like some of the things you are seeing but after we were asked to come in on short notice my men and I will save the west side.

MCALISTER: Are these your concerns or someone else's? Are you just a bit of a puppet, Mr Cooper? You know what to do. Just do it. Fix your approach, get on top of your practices and get your leadership on track. Fix it … It's not about design Mr Stevenson …

STEVENSON: Yes it is.

MCALISTER: It's about people.

STEVENSON: It's not just about people, Mr McAlister. We need those specifications. Now here are your protocol manuals. Read them. Follow them. Dot your i's and cross your t's. Progress defeats pessimism and it builds confidence. Make that your motto.

They all take their protocol manuals on their way out.

COOPER: Look, we do need to get on Mr McAlister, if for no other reason than to finish this job.

MCALISTER: And we will, we will. The drawings will come soon enough lad. Listen to me and we will.

SCENE FOUR

4 p.m., 26 July 1970. The pub.

YOUNG SCRAPPER *is getting beers for* PAT. B.J. *has a transistor radio and a form guide.*

B.J.: Hey, has he still got that little girlfriend?

PAT *turns to see where* YOUNG SCRAPPER *is and moves his hands together to signal that she's gone.*

PAT: Shot through.

B.J. *nods.*

YOUNG SCRAPPER *comes back with the beers.*

B.J.: Did you hear the local primary school kids have been saying the bridge is going to fall down?

PAT: [*to the other* MEN] Here we fucken go. Should've called him radio. He's always had announcements.

B.J. *stares at* PAT *for a moment.*

B.J.: I was down the pub at Newport yesterday. Apparently London's correspondence went to another McIntosh in Newport. A local boilermaker. Don't know what the letters said, but the school kids do.

Everyone laughs.

PAT: The only decent engineer on the job and they hunted him back to London.

B.J.: We should have put more pressure on them to check the bridge out.

PAT *scoffs under his breath.*

PAT: Full of shit.

B.J. *shakes his head and turns up his radio.*

B.J.: Quiet, the horses are in the starters' hands. Okay, come on Reapingtime. He's bred out of Werribee. And he's a beauty.

VICTOR *comes in.*

RACECALLER: [*voiceover*] And they are racing, Harvest Moon has jumped out on the rails. Followed by Deep Sleep with Harry Skidmore on his fourth ride of the day and Reapingtime out of Werribee has settled into third.

They all cheer.

Harvest Moon has been overtaken by Deep Sleep with Reapingtime second and Sandy Bay moving nicely into third. Harvest Chief is slipping through the field with Sansei bringing up the rear. Two hundred metres to go and it's Reapingtime. Reapingtime makes his move.

They cheer louder.

But here comes What a Fella, on the outside. It's What a Fella. What a fella is What A Fella, a hundred to one it's What a Fella punters followed by Sandy Bay, Deep Sleep in third paying two dollars twenty for a place and Reapingtime is fourth by a nose for the quadie.

YOUNG SCRAPPER: You couldn't pick ya own nose. You even backed the doggies on the weekend.

VICTOR: What against the Collingwood? B.J. you crazy, mate.

B.J.: Every loss is one step closer to the perfect bet fellas.

YOUNG SCRAPPER: Tell ya what, Pat, I want it put in the constitution that when the bridge is built none of those eastside fucken Collingwood supporters are allowed over 'ere.

PAT: They might get across the bridge Young Scrapper, but they won't get in. The Spotty's our watering hole. That won't change.

Points to Teddy Whitten's photo on the wall.

Not while we got Teddy on the wall, mate. This is Doggie's country.

B.J.: Thought you couldn't get a start on the bridge?

YOUNG SCRAPPER: Well, tried so many times under me own name and couldn't get on, figured my old man's on top of their blackbanned list. So anyways, I went under a bodgie and bingo, I got on. Was nervous fillin' in the forms but. Thought they might peg me straight away but na, nuthin'.

PAT: What name did you go under?

YOUNG SCRAPPER: Well, that's the problem see, I can't remember what I wrote down.

All laugh.

Ya see it was either Johnson or Johnston. But that made another problem cos I'm supposed to sign somethin' when I get me pay tomorra and I don't want ta give meself up by spellin' me name wrong. I mean I should be able to spell me own name. They wouldn't think we're that dumb, would they?

PAT *laughs and slaps him on the back.*

B.J.: I don't know if you make us all look bad or you make the rest of us look good?

PAT: What did you put down for your first name? I might look that up.

YOUNG SCRAPPER: I used me middle name. It was me granddad's.

PAT: Well, what is it?

YOUNG SCRAPPER: [*mumbling under his breath*] Moystn.

WORKERS: What, what is it? Say it again.

YOUNG SCRAPPER: Moystn, fucken Moystn alright. Can you help me, Pat?

PAT: Sure Moystn, I'll check it out tomorrow for ya. I'll say I'm asking for your details so I can issue you a new union ticket. Should be alright.

YOUNG SCRAPPER: But I already got a ticket. I'm paid up, you know that.

PAT: You have a ticket as Young Scrapper but not this new fella, Moystn.

YOUNG SCRAPPER: I shoulda voted fer Barry Jones.

PAT: You still need another ticket, son.

YOUNG SCRAPPER: Oh fuck. Money's runnin' out my pocket like it's a sieve.

VICTOR *is rubbing his eyes.*

PAT: Now what's wrong with your eyes, Victor? You got a welding flash?

VICTOR: No, it's that black dust. It's everywhere up there. Cuts right into our eyes and it's blowing hard up there today.

B.J.: Even when it's not windy, it's windy up there.

YOUNG SCRAPPER: Gets into me teeth, too.

YOUNG SCRAPPER *tries to show* B.J. *and* PAT *his teeth.* B.J. *brushes him aside.*

B.J.: It's contaminated. Shouldn't even be onsite.

PAT: Hey, don't ya think I know that?

VICTOR: I came to see you about it. I don't want to cause / any trouble.

PAT: No trouble Victor. I want to get some of these issues resolved. We can try and get it moved. Remember, we have to walk if we want anything done round here.

B.J.: Hey, anyone watch TV last night? That Elvis Presley picture that was on? They reckon he can't strum a guitar.

PAT *rolls his eyes.*

YOUNG SCRAPPER: I don't give a flyin' fuck if he can play the guitar or not. I don't want another union ticket, Pat.

B.J.: It's a wellknown fact that when Presley was in the army he didn't sing, only peeled potatoes cos he didn't have his double to play the guitar.

YOUNG SCRAPPER: That young engineer looks like a baby-faced Elvis. Looks about fifteen with his shiny hard hat on. Must go home and polish it.

B.J.: Yeah, he was watching me climb all over the scaffold and doing bolts up one-handed. He was pretty impressed if I don't say so meself, specially being up so high. Wanted me to climb down that gantry ladder. And I wanted to do it, too. We've gotta give and take a bit, you know. But it still doesn't have a rail round it.

PAT: [*snidely*] Did they want your autograph.

B.J.: Fuck off.

YOUNG SCRAPPER: Hey, I'm tellin' the story 'ere. I'm saying, the young engineer's not a bad lad, that's all.

VICTOR: So, you like the engineer more than the wog, uhh?

YOUNG SCRAPPER: Fuck off Victor, that's not my point. He told me that he's been in the office designing sewer ponds. Done it since he left engineering school. So, ya can't go blamin' 'im fer everythin' is what I'm sayin'.

PAT: [*staring at* B.J.] And that ladder's been blackbanned for months and it'll stay blackbanned until they fix it. So don't you go telling them it's dangerous, then suggesting you know a way you could use it.

B.J.: Don't tell me what I can and can't say. You know I know more than half those engineers. School begged me to sign up to the course. And you know it, too.

PAT: Is that your final answer, Barry fucken Jones?

YOUNG SCRAPPER, VICTOR *and* PAT *laugh.*

Okay, I better get home with a few bob in my kick. And you— [*To* YOUNG SCRAPPER] better watch out or you'll blow the shopping money again.

Cheers and drink up for Victor. His missus has another one on the way.

VICTOR: Thanks Pat, yes soon, very soon.

MEN *start to leave.*

B.J.: Don't forget to watch Elvis next time. Watch his left hand and see if he plays the strings.

YOUNG SCRAPPER *and* VICTOR *are left in the pub.*

VICTOR: Come on Young the Scrap, I drive you home.

SCENE FIVE

15 August 1970. West Gate Bridge construction site.

MCALISTER, STEVENSON *and* COOPER *onsite.*

COOPER: Heads up McAlister, there's a lot of heat coming down from the Board.

MCALISTER: Nothing to do with me.

COOPER: I think it's all to do with you. Shit about the job is leaking back to the Westgate Board and it's not from the local primary school either. It's from London.

STEVENSON *enters holding a K-plate.*

STEVENSON: There's hundreds of these malfunctioning angles throughout the boxes. They're twisted, over-stretched. Christ, half of them are not even welded in. Some of them have just been tacked on. What is going on?

You do realise that cars have to drive over this bridge? Every box girder has some plates missing.

COOPER *is drinking a Coke.*

Cooper this is your job. It's not rocket science. And you don't need plans from London.

Turns to MCALISTER.

Who's running this show? You or London?

MCALISTER: I'm my own man, Mr Stevenson. You fooken know that.

STEVENSON: You blindsided me. London reported the failed K-plates to the Board. London did. Why didn't you tell me?

COOPER *and* MCALISTER *are both appealing to* STEVENSON.

MCALISTER: Look, I expected Cooper to rectify things before it got to this. And I only—

COOPER: —They've all been plasticised. They need redesigning.

MCALISTER: What's the point if they're not even welding them in?

COOPER: Yeah, what is the point, Mr Stevenson? We've had two welders working fulltime replacing them and then replacing the ones we replaced. They're a failed extra. It's a joke.

COOPER *drinks his Coke.* STEVENSON *swipes it from him.*

STEVENSON: It's not a joke. And they are not a failed extra. They are crucial reinforcing struts that you, Mr McAlister, should have insisted on being put in correctly.

Looks at both of them.

This job is starting to get away from us … Where are those revised specifications? Or drawings or anything for that matter. And I'm embarrassed to even ask about that bloody Milford Haven report.

MCALISTER: I've requested them. Several times actually. That report will tell us fooken nothing.

STEVENSON: I was so pleased to have you come on board. Your work history's … impressive. But I have to ask, is the job too much for you? Are you under some unseen pressure from London?

If you are, now is the time to speak up.

MCALISTER: I mean Cooper—

STEVENSON *puts his hand up.*

STEVENSON: Don't.

COOPER *twists his can.*

COOPER: —Hold on. We are making deadlines for the first time. I reckon you should be putting a BBQ on for the boys, Mr Stevenson. You know, make something of it?

STEVENSON: I'd hold off on celebrating, Cooper, until you successfully bolt the two, one-hundred-ton steel boxes together, two hundred feet in the bloody air.

I want someone from the design team over here, onsite. Sir John Bancroft, the chief engineer. I want him here, in Australia immediately. And that's hands-on, not down in an office somewhere over in Port Melbourne. Time is not on our side.

MCALISTER: He has retired.

COOPER *laughs.*

STEVENSON: What?

MCALISTER: Retired.

COOPER *stomps his can of Coke.*

STEVENSON: The chief engineer of the bridge retires and you don't say anything?

Then it has to be Rathbone. He led the design team.

MCALISTER: Uhhm.

STEVENSON *drops his head.*

STEVENSON: What's going on?

MCALISTER: He's gone too.

STEVENSON: They've jumped ship?

MCALISTER: I'll contact London and see who's available.

STEVENSON: No you won't. If any more messages come through to the Board from your London office, it will be regarded as a breach of your contract. And don't think I won't sack you, just ask World Services. And Cooper, even London knew your track record on attendance. Stay on the job.

STEVENSON *leaves.*

MCALISTER: Look, I'm sorry it came out as if I grassed you up.

COOPER *laughs.*

COOPER: Listen McAlister, this bridge can fall into the fucking Yarra river for all I care. It's your arse on the line, not mine.

MCALISTER: I just needed to talk to someone who I could trust.

COOPER: Who do you trust, hey?

COOPER *walks out.* MCALISTER *is left alone holding crippled K-plates.*

SCENE SIX

August 1970. Box girder.

YOUNG SCRAPPER *throws all the gear down after hauling it out of one box girder and into another section.*

YOUNG SCRAPPER: [*exhausted*] Where does it say I'm your fucken lackey?

VICTOR: Do you know how much new shield is worth? You don't. You have to look after your tools and keep the work site safe. How does someone like you leave school in this country without an education? Huh.

YOUNG SCRAPPER: What d'ya mean, someone like me?

VICTOR: You have English. You come from England but end up labourer. Can you read or write?

YOUNG SCRAPPER: I can a bit. Sorta.

VICTOR: Why not trade school or university?

YOUNG SCRAPPER: University?

He laughs.

Are you for real? My old man gave me two choices when I turned fourteen. Either be a machinist at Massey Ferguson's or a builder's labourer. He said it was my choice. So I chose this cos I can go steel fixin', scaffoldin', concretin', riggin', even get me crane licence if I wanna go that way. It's better 'an being stuck in a factory all day.

VICTOR: Okay, get that shield over there, Young the Scrap.

VICTOR *gives* YOUNG SCRAPPER *a welding handle.*

Put that rod in it and twist it.

YOUNG SCRAPPER: Hey, I know how to put a rod in the handle. What d'ya think I am?

VICTOR: Okay now look.

VICTOR *puts two old K-plates together and shows* YOUNG SCRAPPER *how to weld.*

You have to melt both sides of the steel into the weld. You savvy.

YOUNG SCRAPPER: I know that. I know more about weldin' 'n you do.

YOUNG SCRAPPER *puts the shield on and off and double-checks the place he needs to start. But he still gets his rod stuck.*

Rips the helmet off.

I'm fucken outta practice. That's all. What are ya tryin' to do? Ya tryin' ta set me up ta look like a dumb arse.

VICTOR: You need a light touch, Young the Scrap. Your hands are too rough. You fuck up the welding and you fuck up the women, huh.

YOUNG SCRAPPER *stops and stares at him.*

YOUNG SCRAPPER: Hey.

Looks over his shoulder.

VICTOR *laughs.*

VICTOR: Don't be too sensitive, huh. Okay, now scrape the rod along the steel a few times and that'll heat up the end. Then try hold the rod just above where you want to weld and let it spark. Then move it slowly. Slowly. Okay. You savvy.

YOUNG SCRAPPER *scrapes the rod and sparks it.*

Look at me.

YOUNG SCRAPPER *looks.*

You safe with me. I be your eyes and ears when you weld. Remember, soft hand.

YOUNG SCRAPPER *takes his shield off.*

YOUNG SCRAPPER: Can you shut the fuck up? I'm tryin' to concentrate.

Puts the shield back on, then starts welding for a few seconds before he loses it. He takes his shield off.

Wow, look Victor, I did it, I did it. Look out, I'll be doin' your job soon. Reckon that's the best weld I've ever done. Have a fucken look at that.

VICTOR: Looks like you spat on it.

YOUNG SCRAPPER: Ya jealous, that's all.

VICTOR: Okay, every time we have a bit of down time, you practise. Huh? And keep that old shield in your kit.

YOUNG SCRAPPER: For me? It's still in good shape too.

VICTOR: Look after it. You look after your tools, your tools will look after you.

VICTOR *moves on and starts knocking some steel with his hammer.* YOUNG SCRAPPER *tidies up, putting his helmet in a safe place.*

SCENE SEVEN

Late August 1970. West Gate Bridge construction site.

B.J. *is measuring up some steel and is looking up at an outer camber web.*

COOPER *enters.*

COOPER: What are you looking at?

B.J.: Look.

Points.

That's buckled, well not buckled, it's hollowed out, isn't it? Like that.

Uses his hand.

COOPER *looks up.*

COOPER: Where? Shit.

Cups his eyes.

B.J.: You've lifted it wrong or something.

COOPER *looks at him as if: 'What would you know?'*

COOPER: That. It's in the design, mate. What do they call you? Barry Jones? It'll pull out when we turn it around.

Looks again.

Actually, it's not as bad as it looks. Bit of an optical illusion there, mate. I think you're thinking too much.

B.J.: It's hollowed out, mate. You can pull a buckle out but you can't pull an inverse hollow out so easily. And fucken … why am I measuring up to restrengthen these joins again?

COOPER: Can you go and get me some angles for the rebracing, and get that lead up here for the welders too?

B.J.: Alright. What about the welder?

COOPER: Yeah, Victor'll need it. Can you crane them up in that small cage? You know the one that … ummm.

B.J.: Yeah of course I know what cage to get. That's my fucken job mate.

COOPER: Great. And I'll get a work order organised for the rest of the material. Thanks.

COOPER *starts to leave.*

B.J.: Hey, did that report come through? About the Milford Haven? Did that …

COOPER*'s gone.*

… come through?

B.J. *stands alone onsite with some leads and angles in his hands.*

SCENE EIGHT

6 a.m. 2 September 1970. Box girder.

Sunrise on top of the bridge. VICTOR *and* YOUNG SCRAPPER *work.*

VICTOR *sings 'Bella Ciao'.*

VICTOR: O partigiano portami via
O bella ciao, bella ciao, bella ciao, ciao, ciao
Stamattina mi sono alzato E ho trovato l'invaser
O partigiano portami via.
O bella ciao, bella ciao, bella ciao, ciao, ciao

YOUNG SCRAPPER: Can you shut the fuck up with ya wog music already?

YOUNG SCRAPPER *gives* VICTOR *a plate to weld.*

I bet ya old man use to sing it, right?

VICTOR: All Italianos sing this song. It's a song of the freedom fighter and his lover. The Italiano is the lover, Young the Scrap. Aussie have no song in them.

YOUNG SCRAPPER: Fuck off.
Sons of the West
Red, white and blue
We come out snarling
Bulldogs through and through

VICTOR: Volare, oh oh
E cantare, oh oh oh oh
No wonder my happy heart sings
Your love has given me wings

Both MEN *laugh.*

YOUNG SCRAPPER: Alright. 'Ere, keep those engineers happy and re-weld these stupid plates. Anyways, why you so happy?

VICTOR *takes his shield off and stops work.*

VICTOR: My wife, my beautiful Frankie, had the baby. Three daughter, now a son. Frankie think she too old to have another baby. But she happy with a boy this time for sure. You have kid?

YOUNG SCRAPPER: Kid? What'd I want a kid fer? Too much trouble anyways. What'd ya call him?

VICTOR: Victor, I call him Victor.

Pause.

YOUNG SCRAPPER: Run outta names, did ya?

VICTOR: My father was Vittorio. And his father and his father's father. Now we have a Victor born in Australia.

YOUNG SCRAPPER: You'll be workin' six days a week till you're a hundred.

VICTOR: I wanna send this boy to the private school over there.

Looks to the east.

YOUNG SCRAPPER: You'll have to rob a bank to send 'em there, mate. Welders' kids don't go there. Them schools are in big old squatters' mansions with swimming pools and tennis courts. Our schools are in dongas for teachin' woodwork and construction. So forget it. And I oughta know, I've been there.

VICTOR: You been there? Bull-a-shit Young the Scrap. As a student?

YOUNG SCRAPPER: Nah, got a few days bumpin' slates onto their roof for repairs.

He laughs.

That's how I know. Told ya, I've been there. But I know B.J. lived over that way for a while.

He laughs.

But he don't talk about it.

VICTOR: I don't want my boy sweating behind mask in the dark all day like me. I want my kids to go to university. And they'll speak good English too.

YOUNG SCRAPPER: Your kids'll end up at Altona tech. Be smokin' by twelve, drinkin' at fourteen, kicked outta school, have a kid and married by eighteen. No-one can read or write at them schools, not even the teachers.

Both laugh.

See those little tinnies going out to sea? That's us. The other mob go rowin', we go fishin'. We follow the bends in the river, mate. They follow straight lines.

VICTOR: You sure you not wog?

YOUNG SCRAPPER: Fuck off.

Both laugh.

VICTOR: Okay, Young the Scrap, you thought a lot about this. I love the fishing too.

YOUNG SCRAPPER: This is our life, Victor, up 'ere workin' on jobs like this. We got site allowances, height allowance and travel money. That's why we gotta keep it low-key, mate. If those shinny arses knew how good we had it, they'd all be tryin' to get a start.

VICTOR *laughs.*

VICTOR: This an unhappy job. Everyone angry. But not today, huh, Young the Scrap, not us, not today.

Look, Melbourne is waking up. See the way the sun sparkles on the water? I like that. It's a good day. A good life. My father he wise to say—

YOUNG SCRAPPER: 'Ere we fucken go. I'm sicka ya old man already and I don't even know him.

VICTOR: Hey, you need listen. Beauty, Young the Scrap, come and go but goodness and kindness last a lifetime. Remember that when you looking for 'nother wife, huh. Maybe the next one won't run away, huh.

YOUNG SCRAPPER: What're ya on about? Run away. Ya think ya fucken Nostradamus now, do ya?

VICTOR *laughs.*

VICTOR: With you? I think I am.

YOUNG SCRAPPER: I can look after meself, mate.

VICTOR: Like when I see you eating that bullshit pie? Frankie cook from our own garden. And we sit outside in summer sometimes, just like she did in her village. But you know, I look and sound Italian but can't remember much. [*Aussie slang*] I'm just a wog from Altona, mate.

YOUNG SCRAPPER *laughs.*

YOUNG SCRAPPER: Yeah, I know what ya mean. Look, see the You Yangs. When I look at 'em they reminds me of Ireland.

VICTOR: But don't you come from England?

YOUNG SCRAPPER: True, but when I'm pissed I sing with an Irish accent. 'Oh Danny boy, the pipes the pipes are calling. From glen to glen and down the mountainside.' The Highlanders.

Fist pump.

VICTOR: Highlanders? That Scotland, isn't it?

Pause.

YOUNG SCRAPPER: Geez, you know how to fuck a story, don't ya? Ya don't get it. I don't feel like I belong nowhere.

VICTOR: I know what you mean. Some people just call us wogs.

YOUNG SCRAPPER: Fair enough. From now I'm callin' you Vittorio, okay.

VICTOR: Okay, good deal. Now Young the Scrap you hold a good tune, huh.

YOUNG SCRAPPER: [*falsely humble*] Na, not really. I was in a pipe band fer a while, ya know.

VICTOR: A pipe band, you?

VICTOR *laughs.*

YOUNG SCRAPPER: Yeah, me. I was good too.

VICTOR: What happen, huh?

YOUNG SCRAPPER *breathes out heavily.*

YOUNG SCRAPPER: Me old man always forgot to pick me up. They'd ask where me mum was and when I said I didn't have one, I got into a fight over it.

VICTOR: Not the mother, huh.

YOUNG SCRAPPER: People looked at me like there's somethin' fucken wrong with me.

VICTOR *pats* YOUNG SCRAPPER *on the shoulder.*

VICTOR: Well, Young the Scrap, now you can tell them that you built this mighty bridge.

YOUNG SCRAPPER: Yeah, you and me Vittorio and seven hundred blokes helped us. That can be our story. One to tell our kids too.

VICTOR: I do tell some people about the bridge, but my wife, shhheeesh. She tell everyone. She says, 'My Vittorio, he work on the bridge they build across the Yarra River'. Even back in Italy everyone talk about me working on this bridge in Australia. So tonight, Young the Scrap, my shout and we drink to the baby. [*In Aussie slang*] A real Aussie born in Altona hospital, mate.

At 7.30 a.m. B.J. *and* PAT *turn up.* PAT *goes over to check a machine.* VICTOR *gathers K-plates and starts measuring up.* YOUNG SCRAPPER *starts unloading form work.*

B.J.: What's all that gear for?

YOUNG SCRAPPER: It's for the form work.

B.J.: Up 'ere? For what?

YOUNG SCRAPPER: For concreting. What else? They are concreting the lot in as part of the underbelly of the road apparently.

PAT: Who is?

COOPER *enters.*

COOPER: My men will be doing it.

B.J.: What was all the extra bracing for? Are you covering up or concreting over?

COOPER: Barry Jones again. It was always in the plans to concrete, so no cover up here.

B.J.: Well, we'll be doing the concreting. You do understand that and form work is a labourer's job, Cooper.

YOUNG SCRAPPER: You got a labourer's ticket?

COOPER: I'm sorry but we're running this job. And as it turns out, I have. And I've had one longer than you. Ya little prick.

B.J.: Hey, watch your manners.

COOPER: In any case, we've been running the carpentry and concrete crews on this job long before any of you got here. What do you think we built this bridge on?

YOUNG SCRAPPER *looks around and sort of acknowledges all the work done prior to the bridge being erected.*

If you want my job, Young Scrapper, go and get qualified. Where'd you go to school? Altona tech or Tottenham High? Did you finish form three or did you get kicked out?

He scoffs.

YOUNG SCRAPPER: Fuck you.

PAT *comes over from servicing a machine.*

PAT: Cooper. This is our turf. Running roughshod over us won't work.

VICTOR, B.J. *and* YOUNG SCRAPPER *all start talking at once.*

VICTOR: —Pat, we shouldn't concrete over the angles and K-plates.
B.J.: —They can't do labouring work when it's our work.

PAT *puts his hand up.*

PAT: Hold it, hold it. Victor—
COOPER: —Makes no difference what he says, this is in the planning. So we are concreting over the plates.
VICTOR: Look at this Pat. Please.

VICTOR *gets a can of Coke, tries to squash the ends and can't.*

You try.

PAT *tries.*

Okay now twist it.

PAT *twists it.*

Okay, now let me do this.

VICTOR *puts a thin alloy strap over it long ways.*

Try now?

PAT *can't twist it.*

Okay. That what the K-plate does.
COOPER: Look, there is enough reinforcement in the joins now. We don't need any more.
PAT: Fair enough, but if you know that, Victor, don't you think ten dongas full of engineers down there would also know that? It has to be safe. Let's sort out this shitshow over whose work it is first.
B.J.: Okay, I want a show a tickets. Right now. They can't be laying any concrete here.

PAT: Settle down, you know full well all Cooper's men have tickets.

YOUNG SCRAPPER: Yeah, they're all fucken rats but. They lag on us to their bosses after the union meetin's.

B.J.: [*to* COOPER] This is how it stands.

PAT: Pull up. I'll deal with this at our onsite meeting.

B.J. *ignores* PAT *and goes finger pointing towards* COOPER.

B.J.: You'll need a fucken builder's labourer's ticket to concrete, a carpenter's ticket to do timber work, a scaffolder's ticket before you touch one fucken pipe or clamp. A steel fixers and ironworkers ticket to do the steel fixing, and a Federated Ironworkers' ticket to operate the fucken derrick.

COOPER: Exactly. Everybody's sitting down waiting for the welder to finish, so the scaffolder can work so the carpenter can work so the concreters can work. These demarcation blues between you blokes have been killing this job.

PAT: Unlike you Cooper, we don't take another man's work. That's our code.

MEN *leave with a stare-off.*

SCENE NINE

15 September 1970. West Gate Bridge construction site.

COOPER *is lifting span 10–11.* MCALISTER *walks in. Two-way argument.*

B.J. *is hooking a load up. There are two different conversations going on.*

MCALISTER: [*from the sidelines, to* B.J.] Fooken risky way to lift it. I can't see how it won't fooken twist lifting it like that.

B.J. *looks up.*

B.J.: [*to* MCALISTER] Know what you mean mate, but you're crossing the line sweetheart. We don't take orders from office jockeys.

PAT *turns up and helps* B.J. COOPER *pulls* MCALISTER *aside.*

COOPER: What'd I say about coming over the top of me like this? You undermine my authority every time you intervene.

MCALISTER: Undermine? You fooken do realise you have to join the other half up on the bridge? My god man, I'm trying to save you from yourself.

MCALISTER *walks back.*

COOPER: [*to* MCALISTER] Smartarse.

MCALISTER: Now there's a couple of ways to do this.

COOPER: Enlighten us, then.

MCALISTER: One: simply disassemble the box and fix the gantry's safety rail on the ground.

COOPER: That'll take weeks. Sorry, it goes up today.

PAT: Look, I think we need to at least put some steel struts in to support the outer camber. So it doesn't twist as well.

COOPER *and* MCALISTER *ignore* PAT.

MCALISTER: Second option is to jack it up. That's what I would recommend under the circumstances. It might take a bit longer but it's probably the safest bet, all things considered.

PAT: Hey, we've been driving cranes for twenty years mate. We know how to lift things.

MCALISTER: [*to* COOPER] How many of these box girders have you lifted so far?

COOPER: About as many as you. You've never built a steel bridge either, have you? The great Rathbone and Watt. You've lived off your reputation and done fuck all. No steel stress calculations, no lifting stress values and no stress levels when the bridge is at full load.

B.J.: What about the bolts under the splice?

COOPER: We'll have to get them from inside the box when it's up in place.

So this is how it stands. We can't do the bolts up because the gantry ladder is blackbanned and we can't fix the gantry up there.

Pulls protocol manual out of his pocket and waves it in the air.

Because of your fucking procedural protocols.

Throws the manual away.

Jack it up then. But this is your call, McAlister, and I want it in writing that you recommended this lifting strategy.

B.J. *discusses things with* COOPER *and* MCALISTER, PAT *is sidelined.*

B.J.: [*to* COOPER] What about we try doing the bolts up under the splice?

PAT: [*to* B.J.] What are you saying? There's no gantry rail on that. You know that.

B.J.: Look, if you lift it without bolting that splice up there is no telling what the boxes will do. It has no fucken diagonal strength.

PAT: Don't fucken start.

COOPER *finally turns to* B.J.

COOPER: Are you saying we can use the gantry ladder?

PAT: No. We can't.

MCALISTER: Could help a lot if—

PAT: [*looks at* B.J.] / No.

B.J.: Give me the bolts. Look, if we climb up there and put every second bolt in, it should make it safer.

PAT: Putting the bolts in don't make it safer for the men. It makes their job easier and we take the risk. We always take the risk for fucken them.

MCALISTER: Back in the day the men rode the fooken jib, Pat. The job came first. This union work to rule is killing us. There's no fooken goodwill on this job. Fooken none.

PAT: It's not a union issue mate. It's common bloody sense.

B.J.: Pat, I know steel, I know lifting. If we lift this without bolting that splice it's a fucken death trap. You understand me? A death trap … for us.

B.J. *starts to go up the gantry ladder.* PAT *stops him.*

Get out of my way, Pat.

PAT *pushes him.* COOPER *intervenes.*

COOPER: Okay, okay leave it. It goes up tonight the way it is. It's McAlister's call.

COOPER *and* MCALISTER *leave.*

PAT: You should get a promotion out of that stunt. You want to go on strike over safety at the meetings and a fucken arse licker in front of the bosses.

B.J.: You don't get it.

Points to splice.

You don't fucken get it. I am thinking of us. Breaking the rules in this case is not breaking the rules.

PAT: Here we go, another smartarse answer.

B.J.: When did you start to fucken hate me? We were best mates once.

PAT: I was your best man once too. But you fucked all that like everything else.

B.J. *is wounded, but can't speak.*

Silence.

They stand, at odds with each other.

SCENE TEN

26 September 1970. Box girder.

YOUNG SCRAPPER: Why do ya keep wearin' those wog shoes to work for? Wearin' 'm out, huh?

VICTOR: They soft on my feet. When I have to weld and squat in tight places my toes get squashed. So sometimes I prefer these shoes.

YOUNG SCRAPPER: Ya too much of a tight arse to throw 'em out.

They laugh. VICTOR *stops work and sits down. Takes one shoe off. Rubs it like an old cobbler.*

VICTOR: Look here, Young the Scrap. See that V. G.? That's my father initials.

YOUNG SCRAPPER: Were they his shoes?

VICTOR: He made them. See the pattern on the front? My father do that by hand. They made for farm work and he walk across Italy in them. My father he say follow the path of Garibaldi to freedom. I've had them re-soled many times. Feel.

YOUNG SCRAPPER *feels.*

YOUNG SCRAPPER: Yeah, but I don't want a pair.

VICTOR: When we came to Australia we live in a little place called Bonegilla and my father suppose to work on the Snowy Mountain Scheme. But mostly they get *the bloody wogs* and take them out to do all the shit jobs the Aussies wouldn't do. Shit pay too. So these shoes have been in many places.

YOUNG SCRAPPER: Not because Frankie won't buy you any boots.

VICTOR *laughs.*

VICTOR: No, not like that …
Shit. Young the Scrap, tape, quick.

YOUNG SCRAPPER *gets the tape and measures out from one end to the other of the two halves of the box girder.* MCALISTER *enters and watches* VICTOR *for a few seconds.*

Okay, go to other corner. This is out of whack. They twist it. Big mistake now.

YOUNG SCRAPPER: I can see that. Maybe I shoulda gone to university.

VICTOR: If they bent the same way, we can. But not like this.

YOUNG SCRAPPER: Who cares? They'll sort it out or they'll concrete over it.

VICTOR: No, this is very serious. You know what bent this? Itself, its own weight bent it. Why didn't they put a brace on?

MCALISTER: Fooken hell, hand me that tape.

MCALISTER *measures up.*

Don't bolt anything yet. I'll get back to you.

MCALISTER *leaves in a hurry. The bridge gives out an almighty scream. Bolts ping, rust lifts.*

YOUNG SCRAPPER: Shiiit, I can see the river through the gap. Look, the sheets are turning blue. Fucken blue.

YOUNG SCRAPPER *grabs hold of* VICTOR, *then starts to run off.*

Fuck this. I'm outta 'ere.

VICTOR: Wait, wait don't leave it like this. Too dangerous. I'm going to see Pat.

PAT *walks in.*

PAT: See Pat about what?

VICTOR: Look, the job's moving all over the place. I thought we going to die.

YOUNG SCRAPPER: That steel went blue in front of our fucken eyes.

VICTOR: You have to tell them, Pat.

PAT: [*to* VICTOR] Relax fellas, you all worry too much. They'll fix it.

SCENE ELEVEN

2 October 1970. Box girder.

MCALISTER *and* COOPER *inspect the box girder with a tape.*

MCALISTER: The camber's twisted.

Shakes his head.

You've really fooked it this time, Cooper.

COOPER: We lifted it the way you advised.

MCALISTER: I didn't tell you to rush it. You supposed to nurse it to the top. I told you before the strength in the design is when it locks in with the other half. You weren't onsite, were you?

COOPER *goes quiet and looks down.*

You fooken bastard.

Calms mindset starting to shift.

Never send a boy to do a man's job.

COOPER: I fucked up. Okay. I'm sorry. I'm being pulled in every fucking direction at the moment. I know it's no excuse. Look, some of my engineers have had a look and think putting a weight on the twisted section should bring it down and we can use the bolts to realign it. It's worth a try at this stage.

MCALISTER: The most important job onsite and you leave it to your juniors. Fook me.

COOPER: The gap is only about four and a half inches in places.

MCALISTER: Try fifteen inches in parts. We're knee-deep in the shit, Cooper, and sinking fast.

COOPER: We have a set of concrete blocks onsite. What about we put them over the bent section? That should flatten it?

MCALISTER: I've never done anything like that before. Unless you take it down and fix it on the ground?

COOPER: That'll put us months behind.

Look, I know we've butted heads on this job, but our best chance now is if we stick together.

We could put the blocks on as soon as the men go home tonight. Could be fixed in a day or two.

MCALISTER: We're in a very precarious position. Every move counts from here on in. You understand me? I'll have to ring London on this one.

COOPER: Why? They threw you under the bus last time.

MCALISTER: Feigning sincerity doesn't suit you, Cooper.

COOPER: Well, it's your call.

COOPER *leaves.*

Light goes on MCALISTER.

MCALISTER: Yeah, it's my call.

SCENE TWELVE

7 a.m., 10 October 1970. West Gate Bridge construction site.

VICTOR, B.J., YOUNG SCRAPPER, MCALISTER, COOPER *find a pyramid of concrete.*

YOUNG SCRAPPER: Hey Vittorio, look, the Pharaohs have been here. Told you they'd concrete somethin'.

VICTOR *goes into the box girder and examines the steel.*

VICTOR: Look, they bloody buckle it now.

They all look at the buckle. The bridge creaks and sways like it is sick. Bolts ping out.

ALL: Fuuuck.

VICTOR, B.J. *and* YOUNG SCRAPPER *look down and see the river again. Feel the bridge move.*

B.J.: We need to get some bolts in the splice, straight away.

MCALISTER *arrives and examines the buckle.*

MCALISTER: Don't touch a thing, you hear?

B.J.: It needs some fucken bolts in, now. What's holding the fucker up?

MCALISTER: Leave it. Don't make out it's worse than what it is.

B.J.: What about the splice? We didn't bolt it up on the ground.

MCALISTER *stares at him.*

MCALISTER: Don't fooken touch it. Now, you've been told.

COOPER *turns up. Looks at* MCALISTER.

COOPER: Okay, you boys can go.
YOUNG SCRAPPER: You don't have to tell us twice.
B.J.: [*yelling back*] You're making a big mistake.
VICTOR: Look, Young Scrap, remember, never follow the first mistake with second mistake.

YOUNG SCRAPPER, B.J. *and* VICTOR *leave the engineers to discuss the buckle.*

MCALISTER *studies the damage. Paces up and down.*

MCALISTER: Fook, fook, fook.

COOPER *looks at the buckle.*

It's fooked.
COOPER: We had to try something.
MCALISTER: Did we?

MCALISTER *is calm, has gone inward. Almost talking to himself now. Working it out on his own.*

Unbolting it should take the pressure off it. If we take some bolts out from the left side and add some on the right side we should be able to pull the twist back. If we can do that, we'll be on our way again.
COOPER: We haven't put the bolts in the splice. If we take these out it would open us up like a T-shape. It's over. I'm calling Mr Stevenson now.

MCALISTER *stares at* COOPER. MCALISTER *continues measuring.* COOPER *follows.*

The gap's too big, McAlister.
MCALISTER: Mr Stevenson? [*Smirking*] He can't fix this. The Board can't and you can't. No. I can fix this.
COOPER: Are you okay? McAlister we need all hands on deck for this. McAlister, McAlister.

Grabs him and shakes him into listening.

Don't do anything, you hear me? Wait. Please. And *don't* take out any bolts.

COOPER *leaves.* MCALISTER, *alone onsite, climbs a ladder, turns and looks out at the bridge.*

MCALISTER: I'm the best fooken bridge builder on this job. Built fooken half the bridges from here to India. I was born on a fooken bridge. Where are those Aussie men? Now take those fooken bolts out.

SCENE THIRTEEN

11:49 a.m., 15 October 1970. Box girder.

VICTOR, B.J. *and* YOUNG SCRAPPER *are in the box girder.* VICTOR *has a hammer gun ready. The bridge moves violently.* B.J. *yells from the top.*

VICTOR: He say take the bolts out.

B.J.: It's fucken moving, get out boys.

It starts shaking violently.

Grab something … hold on.

YOUNG SCRAPPER *is passing a gun to* VICTOR. VICTOR *starts shaking. The bridge is screeching now and the floor is giving way. The bridge pulls apart. The steel screams as it grinds, steel on steel.*

VICTOR: Bolts …

YOUNG SCRAPPER: Fuck the bolts.

VICTOR: Gimme bolt. Quick. Quick.

Bridge shakes.

Run Scrap, run. Get out.

Bridge goes quiet for a moment. Eerie silence. The MEN *come together.*

YOUNG SCRAPPER: Fuck that was close. Let's get out?

VICTOR: I think we should put bolts back. It too dangerous like this. What you think B.J.?

B.J.: I've unloaded this diesel. I'm moving the derrick back to the huts and going for lunch.

B.J. *leaves.*

YOUNG SCRAPPER: Fuck, come on Vittorio. Let's get out of here. McAlister's shouting down the pub.

The two halves of the bridge implode unexpectedly. Sparks fly. The diesel drums are dislodged and start rolling into the imploding hole. Acetylene and oxy bottles roll into the vacuum. The box girder crumbles like thin tin. VICTOR *hangs onto a couple of bolt holes but gets sucked into the hole and falls through the scaffold. Reo bars, wire and steel beams are swinging wildly out of control. There is no orbit. It is chaos.* YOUNG SCRAPPER *holds onto a side of the descending box for what seems an eternity. He is knocked off it. His fall is broken by partially erected scaffolding before he lands on the bottom of the bridge. He can hear water lapping outside and he smells the leaking diesel.* MCALISTER *falls directly down and is hit by a flying steel beam. He dies instantly.*

Inside the rubble of the box girder VICTOR *wakes to find a reo bar speared through his side.* YOUNG SCRAPPER *is beside him, entangled in scaffold. The moment is silent.*

Ohh fuck, Vittorio, Vittorio.

Spits and coughs mouthfuls of dirt and grime out of his mouth.

VICTOR *moans.*

Hey, hey, we're here.

Turns to look at VICTOR.

Vittorio, listen.

Sounds of sirens and crumbling steel and concrete. MEN*'s voices from outside are muffled.*

They'll come fer us, won't they. And we're fucken alive, mate. We're alive.

YOUNG SCRAPPER *gets a piece of steel and hits the wall. Another explosion goes off. Other* MEN *who are trapped start to scream.* YOUNG SCRAPPER *panics and tries to free himself again, with no luck.*

I can't get this beam off me. Can you move?

VICTOR *moans.*

YOUNG SCRAPPER *sees the reo bar that's pierced* VICTOR*'s*

body.

Vittorio, Vittorio stay awake. Please just stay awake.

VICTOR *moves his hand to hold* YOUNG SCRAPPER*'s hand.* YOUNG SCRAPPER *folds his fingers around* VICTOR*'s hand.* YOUNG SCRAPPER *calms. There is quiet.*

YOUNG SCRAPPER *protects himself from another explosion. He hears a knock from outside.*

We're in here, we're in here.

Grabs a piece of bar and knocks on the wall.

They're coming Vittorio. They're coming, mate. Hang on.

VICTOR *dies and* FRANKIE*'s kitchen comes into view.*

YOUNG SCRAPPER *shakes* VICTOR*'s hand and knows he's dead and cries.*

Ya know you were right, my missus shot through and took me daughter. Yeah I got a daughter. I'm gonna find her, yeah. You can meet her too. We'll have lunch at the Spotty. We could do that. Yeah.

Big explosion. VICTOR *and* YOUNG SCRAPPER *are motionless.*

Piling falls down. Blows a hot dust wind over the audience. Stage goes black.

No sound. Lights are flashing, smoke rising, machinery moving.

Transition to outside.

PAT *speaks to imaginary workers. Sirens, smoke, flashing lights.* MEN *screaming. Trucks and machinery sounds in background.*

PAT: You two go down through the West Gate entrance and look for any bodies along the riverbank. And check the muddy edges. Men could still be alive. You two put those barriers up. Oh god. Oh god. That's Ross's jacket. Get a stretcher and move him over the back. You, start digging up the top. And watch yourself. We're not leaving our comrades here. Not like this. Ya hear me—not like this.

PAT *sees an arm in the rubble and clears some debris.*

Quick, help me, there's a body under here. It's McAlister.

PAT *closes* MCALISTER*'s eyes and puts a sheet over him.*

Move him over there. Move all the bodies over there.

MEN *scream from inside the wreck and the steel twists again.*

Scrapper, B.J., B.J., Vittorio.
[*Breaking down*] What have they done?

PAT *squats in the middle of the chaos and it slowly consumes him with machinery, sirens, dust, flashing lights.*

END OF ACT ONE

ACT TWO

SCENE ONE

The lights come up with a kitchen under the rubble. FRANKIE *sits silhouetted inside the kitchen.*

Pause.

YOUNG SCRAPPER *is talking to himself as he takes* VICTOR*'s clothes to* FRANKIE.

YOUNG SCRAPPER, *practising, puts his hand out for a shake.*

YOUNG SCRAPPER: Hi, I'm Scrapper.

Pulls his hand back.

I'll wave: Hi, I'm Scrapper. Don't be a fucken idiot.

Reaches FRANKIE*'s house. He sees the silhouetted head of* FRANKIE *sitting at the kitchen table. Dishes of food on the step. He knocks on the screen door.* FRANKIE *doesn't move. He waits a few seconds.*

Uuh fuck this. Fuck it. Fuck it.

Walks off, walks back, walks off again and stops and looks through the side window. He sees FRANKIE *sitting. He looks at Victor's shoes.*

He knocks on the window and waves.

Hey, fucken oi.

FRANKIE *is unmoved.* YOUNG SCRAPPER *walks away and comes back. And sings:*

Oh, bella ciao bella ciao bella ciao, ciao, ciao.

YOUNG SCRAPPER *sees* FRANKIE*'s head move.*

FRANKIE *turns and looks. Gets up.* YOUNG SCRAPPER *walks back to the door, combs his hair with his hand and pulls his shirt down.* FRANKIE *opens the door. He stops moving.*

They stare at each other. Both nervous, awkward. Silence is palpable. YOUNG SCRAPPER *eventually shuffles and moves under the weight.*

FRANKIE: He love that bloody song.

YOUNG SCRAPPER: I, um, I you know, brought …

YOUNG SCRAPPER *takes out Victor's clothes and shoes to give to her.*

FRANKIE: Nooo, nooo.

She recoils, shakes her head.

Nooo.

FRANKIE *buckles in the doorway.* YOUNG SCRAPPER *is physically upset by her distress.*

YOUNG SCRAPPER *eventually lays Victor's clothes and his shoes on the doorstep and leaves.* FRANKIE *is left sitting on her doorway next to her husband's shoes and clothes.*

SCENE TWO

PAT *and* STEVENSON *speak separately to the workers.* STEVENSON *is holding a piece of paper. The audience act as the workers. Responses are assumed.*

PAT *starts alone on the stage speaking to the audience.*

PAT: Bigmore, Barbuto, Boscolo, Carmichael, Dawson, Eden. [*Crying*] They're all dead. Falzon, Fernandez, Fitzsimmonds, Grist, Gerada, Harburn.

Looks around.

Fucken gone. Westie. [*Upset*] What am I going to tell his kids? He's gone, all gone.

Pause.

Listen up. We've been called in today for an—

Puts his hand up.

I know McAlister said the bridge was safe. But he's dead, he died right in front of me. Look, it's a hard day for all of us.

I don't have any answers. Mr Stevenson is here to tell us where we go from here.

As STEVENSON *stands beside* PAT *there is a pause. It is assumed the* MEN *jeer violently.*

STEVENSON: May I …

Waits.

If you don't mind I will read from a prepared statement.

Waits until MEN *go quiet.*

As a result of the collapse of the Westgate Bridge there will be a Royal Commission into the design failure of Span 10–11 starting on Wednesday the twenty-eighth of October, 1970. Until the reasons for the collapse are understood work will cease, effective immediately.

Pause as STEVENSON *scans the stunned* MEN.

I do appreciate you have spent all weekend pulling your mates' bodies out of the rubble. However—

Pause as STEVENSON *scans the stunned* MEN.

after some negotiations, I have been able to secure, for every man, one week's pay in advance to assist while you look for alternative employment. Those who may want their jobs back when work resumes will be reemployed.

[*Starting to get commanding*] You have until eleven a.m. today to get any of your gear offsite, and henceforth the gates will be closed until further notice. The site is now under formal investigation. Gentlemen, you have one hour.

STEVENSON *leaves.* PAT *stands up.*

PAT: Lads, from here on in we're on our own. So the first thing we're going to do is bury our comrades. And God help me if we don't have one of us at every man's funeral this week.

Pause as PAT *scans the* MEN *and listens to a question.*

Up until last night there were thirty-two dead. Four unaccounted for. I have updates here for those unaccounted for.

Reads from a sheet.

Butters.

Looks up.

He drowned in the mud trapped in that fucken cage. His wife identified his wedding ring. The rats got to him.

Pause.

George burned to death trapped inside the box girder.

PAT *reacts.*

His son identified his tape measure.

Pause.

Fred and Peter were in the safety shed. The bridge landed directly on them. Died instantly.

Pause.

Shovelled them up into a bag.

Pause.

Okay, I want the men remembered as proud working men of the best kind. I don't want the wives and children to hear about their husbands and dads the way we saw them. Ya hear me? That stays with us.

PAT *gathers his emotions.*

Okay. Look.

Studies the sheet.

We'll meet at the Spotty Hotel at ten a.m. every day this week. We'll split up and get to every single person's funeral.

Who'll volunteer to make sure someone gets to Ozelis, Piermarini and Pram's funerals?

Thanks. Can someone look after Suarez, Scarlett and Stewart's?

Thanks.

I still have Tsihilidis and Upsdell. I think Upsdell's family is overseas, so you'll need to check with the police on that one. Anyone?

Thanks. Scrapper will do Vittorio's funeral. I'll take Woods, Wright and West. Jesus, Westie's kids?

Pause.

Alright, we'll meet each morning at the Spotty Hotel to check in. Okay?

[*Repeating the question*] I heard eighteen rode the bridge down and lived. B.J. is on the missing list. His body might never be found.

I saw his derrick go down into the hole. His body wasn't recovered. He lived? He's in hospital.

Nods slowly.

He's alive.

SCENE THREE

YOUNG SCRAPPER *comes up the driveway.* FRANKIE *is folding washing / putting washing on the line. She looks up and walks out to meet him. They size each other up again.* FRANKIE *wins and* YOUNG SCRAPPER *shuffles a little.*

FRANKIE: Who, who you again?

YOUNG SCRAPPER: Scrapper, they call me Scrapper.

FRANKIE: I tell him not to go to work. Stay home do something else but he love that malideto bridge.

YOUNG SCRAPPER: Yeah. Fucken real sorry—

FRANKIE: Sorry, / E allora. So what. He dead. Sorry not bring him back to me.

Studies YOUNG SCRAPPER*'s face.*

You. You the one who ignore me at the bridge. Yes. I call out to you. I ask if you seen my Vittorio but you don't answer. It was you.

YOUNG SCRAPPER: Hey, I just got pulled outta the bridge me fucken self. I didn't—

FRANKIE: —I ask if you seen my husband. I look at you. But you don't answer me. You look away—

YOUNG SCRAPPER: [*yelling*] I didn't wanta say he was, you know, fucken dead.

Silent.

I didn't wanna say he was dead. I didn't want him to be dead. I mean his hand went cold but I didn't know for sure. I mean his hand just went ... That's the last I remember ... until I was pulled out meself.

Silence.

FRANKIE: You speak English.

YOUNG SCRAPPER: Say what? To who?

FRANKIE: You from here. Why don't you speak up? You know something wrong?

YOUNG SCRAPPER: Look, I kept tellin' him to leave. I wanted him to leave. But he wanted to put the stupid fucken bolts back in and then it … the bottom just fell out.

YOUNG SCRAPPER *puts his head down and shuffles.*

FRANKIE: How you live and he die, huh?

YOUNG SCRAPPER: I knew you'd be thinkin' that. I fucken knew it. I don't know. Sometimes I wish I did die.

FRANKIE: —You suppose to look after him. But you don't.

Silence.

[*Angrily*] You suppose to be his eyes and ears. You.

Points.

You suppose to protect him from the danger. That your job. But you don't.

FRANKIE *starts pounding* YOUNG SCRAPPER*'s chest.* YOUNG SCRAPPER *puts up with it for a while. Then* FRANKIE *is just sobbing and* YOUNG SCRAPPER *stops her from hitting him.*

YOUNG SCRAPPER: [*speaks quietly*] I went down with it too. I didn't kill him.

FRANKIE *gathers herself, looks back to see if she has woken the baby. Feels her breasts.*

FRANKIE: I can't, I lose my milk. That baby sleep like his father. I think he know. He sleep like he know something.

YOUNG SCRAPPER: I just brought your car back. I had to move it from the site, you know. It was the last car left in the car park.

Both upset. Silence.

Tries to give FRANKIE *the keys. She won't take them.*

FRANKIE: No. Shhish, cosa ne faccio adesso?

YOUNG SCRAPPER: What?

FRANKIE: What I do with that?

YOUNG SCRAPPER: Well, you know.

Steers with his hands.

Fucken drive it.

FRANKIE: I can't drive it. I can't drive the car. I don't-know-how-to-drive-the-car. [*Upset*] Vittorio always drive the car.

YOUNG SCRAPPER: Well, learn. Get some lessons.

FRANKIE: What, you think I have time? Huh? Four kid, a baby to look after, the shopping. Money? Only Vittorio work, now nothing. We have some saving but not much.

YOUNG SCRAPPER: Sell the fucker then.

FRANKIE: What you talking about? I can't sell Vittorio's car. Shissh.

YOUNG SCRAPPER: Listen, I just got told to move it 'ere, cos they think I know the fucken family.

Throws keys to FRANKIE.

YOUNG SCRAPPER *starts walking off.*

And I'm not takin' the car neither. I gotta go.

FRANKIE: You can't leave Vittorio's car here for me to see. To remind me. Every day.

YOUNG SCRAPPER *walks off.*

You have cold heart. A cold heart.

FRANKIE *is left holding the keys and washing basket. Kicks the door open with her foot. Looks up as if she is talking to* VICTOR *and goes inside.*

SCENE FOUR

27 October 1970. COOPER, STEVENSON. *Engineers convene a meeting on the east side.*

COOPER: What happens now? Do you think the police will get involved?

STEVENSON: No, not with a Royal Commission. The coroner's report is where the law could intervene. But I am led to believe by our legal team that the most likely outcome will be a finding that men died by 'misadventure' and that will clear us of any wrongdoing.

COOPER: Misadventure? Sounds like they died on a fishing trip.

STEVENSON: Mistakes were made. We all accept that. A measure of responsibility is the tone. Now if we are to salvage our careers and our firm's reputation then we must follow the facts.

COOPER: A measure of responsibility? Even my wife is sort of on the men's side. Well the families, the children really.

Pause.

She went to one of the men's funerals, said it was bad. I said you don't know what the men were like to deal with. And, and McAlister was an obstinate … daft know-all.

STEVENSON: McAlister … He came with such promise and gusto.

Pause.

Born on a bridge and died on one.

COOPER: Did you speak to the family?

STEVENSON: No, no I didn't. I did write a letter offering my condolences. It wasn't received too well. How do you explain … this catastrophe was always a matter of when not if.

COOPER: I had to inform Shaw's mother. She told me he was dux of his engineering class. She said I sent him home from work in a coffin.

STEVENSON: Yes, such promise. A great loss to engineering too. Still, we accept bridge building is not a precise science. Cutting edge designs and techniques comes with risks. We learn, we grow and we adapt.

COOPER: Are you going to say that at the Royal Commission? Cos no-one is going to buy it. We are fucked. Any way you look at it, there's no way out of this.

STEVENSON *picks up paper and shakes it.*

STEVENSON: We have our own documented paper trail. That will be our eyes and ears from here on in. Facts. Verifiable facts. In any case, they will only be investigating the design failure in span 10–11 specifically of the North-South box girder 4–5 join on the actual day of the bridge collapse.

COOPER: That's specific.

STEVENSON: It gives us a pretty good hand to work with.

COOPER: Well McAlister went rogue. I think that is pretty obvious.

STEVENSON: Forget scapegoating him. Rathbone and Watt will not let one of theirs go down.

COOPER: What about all the drawings and calculations that never arrived. Where are they?

STEVENSON: Missing.

COOPER: Missing?

STEVENSON: We believe the drafting team took them when their contracts finished. In any case we have no evidence of that type to submit.

COOPER: We are finished then.

STEVENSON: One has to have evidence to be found guilty, Cooper.

COOPER: What about when we concreted over the K-plates? That was a cover up.

STEVENSON: It was just a modification. Part of ongoing adjustments to procedures. Nothing incriminating there.

COOPER: [*reading report*] 'The October twenty-second report is damning. If the bridge was rebuilt to the present design it would be to the level of satisfactory'. Are you kidding me? Who wrote that? You.

STEVENSON: We commissioned a subsidiary of our firm to do the report because we didn't trust an independent assessor. It's that simple.

COOPER: After the Milford Haven collapse, you and McAlister promised those men at that meeting an independent report on the bridge's safety.

STEVENSON: And we have a report.

COOPER: Can you hear yourself? The report came in seven days after the bridge collapsed and it said the bridge was safe?

STEVENSON: And that is evidence we will submit to the Royal Commission.

COOPER: It fucking collapsed. The bridge is rubble. Thirty-five men died. An independent report could have saved lives.

STEVENSON: Could haves, would haves, should haves are not evidence.

Pause.

We have evidence in our hand that the calculations were in the range of satisfactory. Written by experts. This report doesn't make us right, but it doesn't make us wrong.

COOPER *puts his head down.*

It's cruel I know, but the law is cruel. Not us.

COOPER: What about McIntosh? You won't shut him up.

STEVENSON: Unfortunately, he is hiking somewhere in the Lake District and cannot be contacted.

COOPER: The community will see through this ruse.

STEVENSON: The Royal Commission is not about what happened. It's about what can be proven and what cannot be proven.

COOPER: So we do have a get-out?

STEVENSON: We have a defence and a good one I would have thought. What do you think?

SCENE FIVE

FRANKIE *is in the outside laundry. Surrounded by a basket of washing, ironing and a broom and mop. Puts her hands on her hips and lifts her head.*

YOUNG SCRAPPER *comes around the corner.*

FRANKIE: Another man. How many more come from the bridge today?

YOUNG SCRAPPER *looks around.*

I just have Welfare man from the bridge here. He check my housework before the allowance come. He sees all my washing baskets. Wants me to keep the house a 'little cleaner'. He say my house don't smell too bad for migrant.

Crunches her fist up.

I want to kill this man.

He pick up Vittorio's shirt from under my pillow. He like Columbo. He look everywhere. When he sees the shirt, he think he found the gun.

He say 'You have a boyfriend?' Because you can't get allowance if you have the man, you know.

But I say, 'No. You know anyone want migrant widow with four kid?' I rip it off him. Say, 'Don't touch my husband shirt.'

She sniffs a shirt in her hand.

That all I have left of him ... Now, I really want my own money. A job. I know I have three kid and a baby, but so what. Now I have to be man and the woman. And I do have chance for job at meatworks.

Not perfect but two bus rides away and I really sick of bus. I really hate carry shopping home on bus, I hate that.

YOUNG SCRAPPER: Ya gotta car there. Drive it.

FRANKIE *looks awkwardly at the car.*

YOUNG SCRAPPER *grabs the broom, shoebox and tissue boxes.*

Look, ya worryin' 'bout fucken nuthin'. I'll show ya. Come sit down. Okay, three pedals. That's the clutch. The brake and the accelerator. This is the gear stick. It's like a H, okay? One, two, three, four, reverse. But we won't worry 'bout that last one yet.

FRANKIE *rolls her eyes.*

FRANKIE: Alright, I suppose I can learn pedal.

YOUNG SCRAPPER: Okay, when I say which pedal you put your foot on it.

FRANKIE: Okay.

YOUNG SCRAPPER: Clutch.

FRANKIE *presses the brake.*

YOUNG SCRAPPER: —Nooo, that's the brake. Clutch is left. Brake—

Points.

—and accelerator is that one.

FRANKIE *practises a few times.*

Ya right.

FRANKIE: I got it.

YOUNG SCRAPPER: Okay. Ready? Brake.

FRANKIE *presses the accelerator.*

Noooo.

Clasps his hands on his head, stresses.

That's the fucken accelerator. [*Screaming out*] You'll kill somebody like that.

FRANKIE: [*blowing up*] I not kill no-one, not like you.

YOUNG SCRAPPER *stares.*

YOUNG SCRAPPER: Hey, I fucken didn't kill Vittorio. Stop bringing that up. Get over it. I was with him. So don't fucken tell me what happened when you weren't there. You always say Vittorio loved life, well you should try it. You're suckin' fucken oxygen, aren't ya?

Silence.

He was always fucken with my head, him and his salami and grappa. And his old man's sayin's.

He laughs.

I don't know how he knew 'bout me girlfriend leavin' me. I told him 'bout me daughter too. Told him I'd find her. And I will too.

FRANKIE: You have daughter? Where she?

YOUNG SCRAPPER *shrugs his shoulders.*

FRANKIE *is pulled out of her pity.*

So, you have some family?

YOUNG SCRAPPER *nods.*

YOUNG SCRAPPER: Somewhere.

FRANKIE: Want some Vittorio's grappa, huh?

YOUNG SCRAPPER: Na, I'm off the piss now.

FRANKIE: Mmmm, off the piss, then you should find your daughter, Mr Scrap. Huh?

YOUNG SCRAPPER: Maybe … I gotta go. We're all meetin' back at the West Gate today. See what happens.

YOUNG SCRAPPER *starts to leave.*

FRANKIE: Ciao, then.

YOUNG SCRAPPER *laughs.*

YOUNG SCRAPPER: Bella fucken ciao, huh.

FRANKIE *watches him leave.*

FRANKIE: Find your daughter Mr Scrap.

SCENE SIX

COOPER: Thank you for meeting with us.

PAT: Can you imagine what would happen if any of the boys saw us?

COOPER: Let me get straight to the point then Pat. They want to offer you a job … with us.

PAT: —Fucken forget it, mate.

COOPER: Hear me out, Pat, just hear me out. I can't leave here without your signature mate. That's how much they want you.

PAT *laughs.*

PAT: I'd be fucken crucified. Jesus got taken off the cross mate, I never would.

COOPER: Yeah okay. But you would be employed by us as a leading hand, still dealing with the men. Still with your friends but working for us.

PAT: Can I bring Scrapper and B.J. with me?

STEVENSON: Pat we could put you on another site for a while until you find your feet. Now—

PAT: What about the boys?

COOPER: We are offering fifty dollars a week more than you are earning now, a car, superannuation, a phone account and it's a job for life. Your family would be secure.

PAT: All or no-one mate.

STEVENSON: B.J. and Scrapper won't be back, mate.

PAT: What? We were fucken promised. Stevenson promised us onsite. Right where the men died.

COOPER: He did. But the powers to be are deadset worried there will be recriminations. We're all better off with a clean slate.

PAT: Did you get your job back?

PAT *leaves. There is a sheet and a pen left on the bench.*

SCENE SEVEN

Mid-June 1971.

Sign on entry gate says West Gate.

PAT *is at the work site at dawn, before it opens. He is nervously waiting for* B.J. *He comes round the corner on his walking stick and with a bit of a claw hand. They haven't spoken since the collapse.*

PAT *and* B.J. *look at each other for a few minutes as* B.J. *hobbles towards* PAT. PAT *is nervous and fidgety.* B.J. *is smiling, pleased to see him.*

B.J.: Why are we here so early?

PAT: Look, I wanted to talk to you before the others got here.

B.J.: Forget it, Pat, fuck me.

PAT: Look, a lot's happened but I need to say, you know, I shouldn't a said those things.

B.J.: Yeah. Look you don't have to—

PAT: Can you shut the fuck up for a minute? I'm trying to get a few things out here.

B.J.: Pat. Sitting in the hospital … I been thinking about a lot of shit. You were right about a lot of things.

Silence.

PAT: I'm sorry I didn't visit you either. Wasn't sure, you know …

B.J.: I didn't really want visitors except nurses.

PAT: Fuck me, I've known you longer than anybody. And we've been best mates since I can't remember when. I should of, you know …

B.J.: Ahh, it's alright.

PAT: Stop saying that. I need to get this shit out. I thought you were … fucken dead mate. When I found out you were alive I … well I realised.

B.J. *nods.*

B.J.: Yeah I know what you mean.

PAT: You do?

B.J.: Yeah I get it.

PAT: I just needed to tell you that.

B.J.: It means a lot hearing it from you Pat. Now will you shut the fuck up?

PAT: Have you, you know, heard from her? None of my business anyway.

B.J.: No, haven't mate and I'm sort of glad. This is on me.

PAT: Is this the bit where we kiss?

B.J. *tries to hit him with his walking stick and* PAT *takes a blow before grabbing it. They have a little wrestle.*

B.J.: Get off me, ya prick.

PAT: There is something else I have to talk to you about.

B.J.: You know when my derrick fell into the hole, I thought I was gone.

PAT: How the fuck did you survive?

B.J.: When it started sliding into the hole I climbed over the back of it and hung on, thinking I'd be safer there. When it tipped it catapulted me into the air. They reckon I was two hundred feet up. Landed on the elevated wire mesh down where they build the boxes. My steel trampoline saved me.

PAT *shakes his head.* YOUNG SCRAPPER *walks in.* PAT *and* B.J. *are really happy to see him. Shake hands and* YOUNG SCRAPPER *punches* B.J. B.J. *hits him with his walking stick. They laugh.*

YOUNG SCRAPPER: They couldn't fucken kill you, could they. How ya going, mate?

B.J. *tries to hit him with his walking stick.* YOUNG SCRAPPER *laughs.*

B.J. *looks at the time.*

What happened?

B.J. *puts his hand on* YOUNG SCRAPPER*'s shoulder.*

B.J.: I'll tell you later, Young Scrapper. Where are the bosses? Are you sure I'll get put on again? Like this?

PAT: Guaranteed, mate.

YOUNG SCRAPPER: What about me? Ya sayin' I won't have any trouble gettin' on? I mean, I shouldn't but I don't believe it.

B.J.: Well, if I can get on with one hand and one claw you should be a shoo-in, mate.

They head over to the West Gate entrance. It is locked.

PAT: That's the road back to hell, boys.

YOUNG SCRAPPER: Well, hell'll have to wait. We're locked out before we even start. That's a record.

B.J.: Is it the right day? Was the return to work today?

COOPER *marches out with a clipboard. He is more assertive than before.*

YOUNG SCRAPPER: 'Ere we go. There's no way he's gonna put me back on.

COOPER: Gentlemen.

PAT: Cooper.

B.J. *and* YOUNG SCRAPPER *both nod.*

YOUNG SCRAPPER: G'day.

COOPER: Can I talk to you, Pat?

PAT: It's all of us or the job doesn't start.

YOUNG SCRAPPER: What's with the secret meeting? We're fucked, aren't we?

COOPER *looks awkward.*

B.J.: Or something else.

COOPER *is quiet for a moment.*

COOPER: Well, we are starting off slowly fellas.

PAT: 'Starting off slowly', that's a new one.

YOUNG SCRAPPER: I, I, what else are we gonna do? What about our boys who died?

COOPER: We are starting off casual until we get going.

B.J.: Who, who's going to give me a fucken job? I'm a right fuck-up, but I thought you know, we might get …

PAT: Where's Stevenson?

COOPER: Stevenson … He's been recalled to London.

YOUNG SCRAPPER: Another one gone.

COOPER: He's been reassigned. In fact he's the new President of Engineers in London.

PAT: Fuck me.

B.J. *limps up to* COOPER.

B.J.: You can disappear, erase us from your memory or your work history, but we won't forget what happened. Not here mate.

COOPER: Pat, you can go in. I'm sorry B.J. Nothing personal but you're a cripple mate. And Scrapper, there's nothing here for you either. Get a fresh start, mate.

YOUNG SCRAPPER: What, in fucken London?

PAT: Hang on, B.J. can drive the derrick in the yard and load and unload trucks.

YOUNG SCRAPPER: He knows more about the job than you do. He told you about bolting up the splice and you didn't listen. Well, what's your excuse with me, then?

COOPER: Did you read any of the Royal Commission … The judge explicitly said one of the factors in the catastrophe was the men's militancy and ongoing demarcation disputes. You, all of you, have to take your share of responsibility for the men's deaths. We don't want that militancy back. And you Scrapper, you'd go on strike if the urn's not hot.

YOUNG SCRAPPER: Well, keep it fucken hot, mate.

PAT: It's all of us or none of us, Cooper. What do you want?

COOPER: I have my orders, Pat, only you.

MEN *get in a huddle.*

PAT: I know we're all skinned but we need to shut the job down, straight away. We need a picket line.

YOUNG SCRAPPER: I'll get some drums and a rope. When Monday comes we'll be ready.

PAT: Okay, I'll contact Trades Hall and get the strike sanctioned.

B.J.: I'll call some of our bludging politicians. Put a bit of pressure on Bolte.

Okay, Cooper, see how the Premier goes with a front-page story: 'Survivors locked out of their jobs'.

SCENE EIGHT

FRANKIE *and* YOUNG SCRAPPER *meet on the house steps. They nod at each other.*

FRANKIE: What, no driving lessons?

YOUNG SCRAPPER: Nah. Ya nearly killed us last time.

FRANKIE: That stupidio man nearly ran into me.

YOUNG SCRAPPER: You were on the wrong side of the road. And you pressed the accelerator a-fucken-gain instead of the brake. Ya too dangerous. Look not everyone's a natural when it comes to drivin'.

Pause.

FRANKIE: I don't like it when you say I can't drive. Look, I got you this for helping me.

YOUNG SCRAPPER: What's this?

FRANKIE: Read it. These are the words Vittorio sing. You know we all grow up with 'Bella Ciao' and Vittorio, he loved to hear his father sing it.

It a story of an intruder coming between a good man and his lover and he is saying goodbye to her. He tells her if he gets killed he want to be buried in the mountain under the beautiful flower. When people pass him by he say they will say, 'Oh what a beautiful flower. ' Mr Scrap, Vittorio is my beautiful flower.

YOUNG SCRAPPER *and* FRANKIE *have a silent moment.*

YOUNG SCRAPPER: I still have the same nightmare about us trapped.

YOUNG SCRAPPER *pauses.*

Sorry … Sorry I shouldn't—

FRANKIE: —No. Go on. Please. No-one will tell me what really happened. Even the other man won't tell me. I want to hear what happened to him. How he die? Please? How he die?

YOUNG SCRAPPER: Well, when the bridge moved … he tried to put the bolts back in but it was too late. And the bridge opened up and just fucken swallowed us inside. Next thing we were covered in dust and fucken diesel. He had a reo bar through his side. And I was trapped under scaffold. Then the diesel exploded and we thought we would be burned alive.

FRANKIE *quietly sobs.*

FRANKIE: Go on.

YOUNG SCRAPPER: I told him to hang on, you know.

FRANKIE: Did he … did he say anything … about me?

Silence. YOUNG SCRAPPER *looks up and sees* VICTOR *holding the baby in the kitchen.* VICTOR *looks at him.*

YOUNG SCRAPPER: Yeah. Yeah he did. It was hard for him to speak because he had that reo bar in his guts, but he was still fucken talkin' 'bout you.

FRANKIE: Well, come on, what he say?

YOUNG SCRAPPER: He said …

Pause, looks up and sees the kitchen and that VICTOR *is looking at him.*

He said, 'Beauty comes and goes but goodness and kindness last a lifetime'. He said 'That's my bella'. Yeah.

Pause.

FRANKIE: He say that? He would say that too you know because that what his father say and Vittorio just want to be like his father.

YOUNG SCRAPPER: Yeah.

FRANKIE: What else?

YOUNG SCRAPPER: He said I should try and marry someone like you.

FRANKIE: [*laughing*] Bravo, bravo, Vittorio. Thank you, thank you. Bravo.

She cries and laughs. YOUNG SCRAPPER *reaches out and holds her hand.*

He reached out and held my hand, you know … that's when he died. That's the last thing I remember.

FRANKIE: Thank you … this sounds stupid, I know but one time I follow the man at the supermarket who I think look like Vittorio. Until I see his face. Then I think I'm forgetting him.

Silent.

Some evening I walk to his fishing spot. When I get close my heart beats as if I will see him. I never get to say goodbye to him. The bridge take my part … my good man. My husband. Like that he's gone.

Silence.

Now what about you, you find your daughter?

YOUNG SCRAPPER: She don't seem interested in seein' me.

FRANKIE: Maybe write a letter.

YOUNG SCRAPPER: And say what?

FRANKIE: Well don't write about the bloody bridge.

He laughs.

Don't be too serious. That like hitting the accelerator instead of the brake.

YOUNG SCRAPPER: Yeah, I get it.

But he doesn't.

I can't spell neither. You think that matters?

FRANKIE: Of course. You have to show you care, that the main thing.

YOUNG SCRAPPER: Okay.

FRANKIE: Hey, what you say?

YOUNG SCRAPPER: What? [*Whispering*] Fanks.

FRANKIE *maintains her stare.*

[*Louder*] Fucken fanks.

FRANKIE *nods and smiles.*

What 'bout you sayin' sorry for blamin' me?

YOUNG SCRAPPER *turns to walk off.*

FRANKIE: Little steps for a broken heart, Mr Scrap. Little steps.

SCENE NINE

Morning comes and YOUNG SCRAPPER *has fire drums set up, and a rope across the entrance as the picket line.*

B.J.: Good job, Scrapper. There she is.

The West Gate entrance sign.

One more dance with the devil.

YOUNG SCRAPPER: Sometimes me and Vittorio would be on top of the bridge when the sun comes up like this. I've missed that. We were on top of the world back then.

B.J.: Singing on the bridge?

YOUNG SCRAPPER: You heard us.

He laughs.

The MEN *look at each other.*

YOUNG SCRAPPER *and* VINNY *laugh.*

YOUNG SCRAPPER *nods.*

It's been a while.

B.J.: I don't know how I feel about going back onto the bridge …

YOUNG SCRAPPER: Me neither.

B.J.: I didn't want to live when I saw my hand, you know … There was a time I thought I couldn't get any lower. Did you know a few years ago I lost everything?

YOUNG SCRAPPER: Everyone knew.

B.J.: You knew me missus shot through?

YOUNG SCRAPPER *nods.*

And I blew over a hundred grand on one race?

YOUNG SCRAPPER: Well you didn't come back here because ya fucken missed us, did ya?

B.J.: Fuck it. I'm busted though, been borrowing money from my fucken mother, feel so ashamed of myself.

YOUNG SCRAPPER: You're alive mate. And tou—[gh]

B.J.: —Hey don't steal my thunder mate. You just gotta listen and nod. That's in the rule book.

They laugh.

YOUNG SCRAPPER *nods.*

Where was I? Yeah I was feeling black then I switched. Don't know how it happened. I didn't get religion or anything. But I felt different. I just realised what you said. I'm alive. Everything's a bonus from here. When I wake up I tell myself I've been given a second chance at life. That gets the blankets off me. Then I put my socks on. Then I put my shoes on. Then I make a cuppa. I do that every day.

YOUNG SCRAPPER: Can I talk now, or what?

B.J.: Yeah.

He laughs.

Off you go.

YOUNG SCRAPPER: Ya gotta find your song mate.

B.J.: What?

YOUNG SCRAPPER: You know, sing. From the fucken … heart.

B.J.: What the fuck are you talking about?

YOUNG SCRAPPER *picks up a page with the lyrics to 'Bella Ciao'.* B.J. *grabs it.*

What're ya trying ta read?

Looks over.

That's not English.

YOUNG SCRAPPER *starts trying to play the bagpipes.*

B.J.: You can't play the pipes and ya can't fight either.

YOUNG SCRAPPER: I'm practisin' and I'm learnin' Italian. Ya gotta problem with that?

B.J.: You going to Italy?

YOUNG SCRAPPER: Na.

B.J.: What are ya trying to do then?

YOUNG SCRAPPER: [*angrily*] I'm trying to be, you know, not so fucken angry, that's all. Learn to sing … from the heart. Smell the fucken flowers mate.

B.J. puts his arm round YOUNG SCRAPPER, squeezes him and kisses his head. PAT arrives and they all warm themselves. PAT turns up.

B.J.: So what's going on Pat? Where's Cooper?

YOUNG SCRAPPER: Is there a meeting?

PAT: I got told there was.

Voices start coming from behind the West Gate. It is dark. PAT goes closer to the gate.

Listen. I can hear someone coming.

Voices get louder.

COOPER comes out of the dark, dressed in suit and tie with hard hat on.

It's Cooper.

YOUNG SCRAPPER: 'Bout time, hey.

COOPER: Gentlemen. I'll read from a prepared statement. 'Against the direct advice of both the consulting and construction engineering firms the Westgate Board have been instructed by the government to reinstate all employees who lost their jobs as a result of the collapse. Effective immediately.'

All the MEN yell.

YOUNG SCRAPPER: Is that it?

COOPER: That's it.

YOUNG SCRAPPER: So we won.

COOPER: Nobody won. Report onsite through the West Gate.

COOPER retreats and leaves.

Darkness descends. Voices emerge and get louder.

VOICE 1: [*offstage*] Ya can't sit on ya arse all day.

B.J.: That sounds like Westie.

Voices get louder. MEN line up on the edge of the darkness.

VOICE 2: [*offstage*] What da'ya want, a personal invitation?

VOICE 3: [*offstage*] Get your arse into gear.
VOICE 4: [*offstage*] Finish the fucker.
VOICE 5: [*offstage*] Don't let those shiny arses get the glory.
VOICE 6: [*offstage*] What have ya hands gone soft? Come on, get back to fucken work.
VOICE 7: [*offstage*] This is our bridge. Finish it.

The voices overlap and build to a crescendo. VICTOR *emerges from the darkness, dressed and injured as he was when he died. He opens the West Gate.*

Light goes on the West Gate entrance sign. The MEN *hold hands and walk back to work. Lights go on.*

B.J. *hops in a crane.* PAT *starts grinding and* YOUNG SCRAPPER *starts hammering some steel. Machine noise, smoke, sparks, reversing beeps and warning lights go on. A large piling is lifted into place and a hot gust of wind blows over the audience. Darkness follows and then the erected piling is in place.*

B.J. *blows his whistle.*

Silence.

SCENE TEN

YOUNG SCRAPPER, B.J., PAT, *sitting around looking at the bridge piling in span 10–11.*

YOUNG SCRAPPER: Do you think the others'll come?
PAT: Well, they all put in for the grog so they'll be here.
YOUNG SCRAPPER: What about Frankie?
PAT: Did you ask her?
YOUNG SCRAPPER: Yeah. But she said she'd never come to this place.
PAT: Well … up to her.

A car screeches in and the brakes squeal. The MEN *stop and look at each other.* FRANKIE *enters, carrying Victor's shoes.*

FRANKIE: Shit the fuck.
B.J.: Frankie's here.
FRANKIE: Good morning, gentlemens.

FRANKIE *stands under the intimidating piling and feels her heart.*

So this is where they took my Vittorio.

YOUNG SCRAPPER: You're just in time.

PAT *goes over and opens the curtain to the plaque.*

B.J. *goes over. He touches every name on the plaque.*

YOUNG SCRAPPER: That doesn't look square to me.

B.J.: You're cock-eyed, that's all.

B.J. *brings out a few beers. The* MEN *sit down.*

PAT: Okay, we can't do this without a few beers so wrap ya gob around these.

Everyone has a drink. YOUNG SCRAPPER *pours tea from his thermos.*

I'm glad you came Frankie because this might be the last time we're all together.

FRANKIE: Why, where you go Pat?

PAT: Me, I got on as one of the conveners down at Portland's new smelter.

B.J.: Well done.

PAT: What's about you, B.J.?

B.J.: Me, I'm heading north. Warmer weather. Better for me injuries. Got offered a start on some high-rises, so I took it. Got some family up the Gold Coast too.

PAT: Got a new woman up there?

B.J. *laughs.*

B.J.: Who wants a man with a claw?

PAT: Good point.

YOUNG SCRAPPER: Well, I'm givin' it a go. Me missus wants ta marry me. And we're havin' a kid too. Anyway, got life without parole, mate. Next I'm gonna build an aviary.

B.J.: What with little birds in it?

YOUNG SCRAPPER: Well, that's what an aviary fucken is, B.J.

B.J.: See what happens when you stop drinking? It plays with ya head.

FRANKIE: And Mr Scrap what about?

YOUNG SCRAPPER: … Yeah, yeah I been seein' me fucken daughter.

FRANKIE: Did you take her for lunch, huh?

YOUNG SCRAPPER: Fish and chips down the pier. She liked the fish more'n she liked me.

PAT: How are your kids, Frankie?

FRANKIE: The older ones they part Aussie, they don't do homework. Part Italian, they always going down that Altona pier, but no fishing. But my young Victor, ohh he smart a boy. He numero uno. He get good education and become a welder just like his father and his father's father.

YOUNG SCRAPPER: Are ya workin'?

FRANKIE: Yes. [*Proudly*] I on the line packing meat. T-bone, scotch fillet, rump, hamburger. Don't eat hamburger. Full of pigs' ears, cows' tails, sawdust. Everything go into mincer. We get to take meat home, too. Not hamburger. The boss say we can all cheat a little bit, but not too much.

He laughs.

He tries a little bit with me too. Because I a widow he thinks, you know, boom, boom. I say forget it, mister, you can never have my hamburger.

MEN *laugh.*

YOUNG SCRAPPER: Are we ready for this?

PAT *and* B.J. *go arm in arm.*

FRANKIE: [*holding her heart*] I think one day I am going to be ready … to let go, but not true. The pain is for my soul to keep.

Pause. Turns to the audience.

And look, I even got bloody tattoo.

Lifts up one arm.

This one is Victor.

Lifts up other arm.

This one the Westgate. As long as people ask me, I keep telling his story. We not forgot him.

PAT: It's time.

They all stand for a minute's silence. FRANKIE *walks over, rubs Victor's shoes on her cheek, kisses them and puts them under the plaque. The spotlight goes onto the shoes.*

At the end of a few moments YOUNG SCRAPPER *stands to sing 'Bella Ciao', a cappella style.* FRANKIE *joins in then the* MEN. *The audience are invited to sing. A last tribute to* VICTOR.

ALL: Stamattina mi sono alzato
E ho trovato l'invaser
O partigiano portami via.
O bella ciao, bella ciao, bella ciao, ciao, ciao
O partigiano portami via che mi sento di morir
E se io muoio da partigiano
O bella ciao, bella ciao, bella ciao, ciao, ciao
Stamattina mi sono alzato
E ho trovato l'invaser
O partigiano portami via.

THE END

NEXTSTAGE

Developed through Melbourne Theatre Company's NEXT STAGE Writers' Program with the support of our Playwrights Giving Circles.

NEXT STAGE positions new Australian works as contenders on the national stage, through strategic investment in stories that reflect our community, are relevant to our times, challenge the boundaries of theatre making and fuel the cultural conversation.

Thank you for sharing our passion and commitment to Australian stories and Australian writers.

PLAYWRIGHTS GIVING CIRCLE

Thank you to Melbourne Theatre Company's Playwrights Giving Circle – its donors, foundations and organisations – for sharing our passion and commitment to Australian stories and writers.

Tony & Janine Burgess, Fitzpatrick Sykes Family Foundation, Jane Hansen AO & Paul Little AO, Larry Kamener & Petra Kamener, Susanna Mason, Prudence & Neil Morrison, Helen Nicolay, Pimlico Foundation, Tania Seary & Chris Lynch, Craig Semple, Dr Richard Simmie, Andrew Sisson AO & Tracey Sisson, Derek Young AM & Caroline Young

Melbourne Theatre Company

BOARD OF MANAGEMENT

Chair
Martin Hosking
Deputy Chair
Leigh O'Neill
Tony Johnson
Larry Kamener
Katerina Kapobassis
Suzie Miller
Chris Oliver-Taylor
Tiriki Onus
Anne-Louise Sarks
Craig Semple
Professor Marie Sierra

FOUNDATION BOARD

Chair
Craig Semple
Deputy Chair
Jane Grover
Karen Cusack
Charles Gillies
Sally Lansbury
Anne-Louise Sarks
Rupert Sherwood
Tracey Sisson

EXECUTIVE MANAGEMENT

Chief Executive Officer & Artistic Director
Anne-Louise Sarks
Executive Producer & Deputy CEO
Martina Murray

ARTISTIC

Artistic Administrator
Olivia Brewer
Associate Artists
Jean Tong
Mark Wilson
Head of New Work
Jennifer Medway
New Work Associate
Zoey Dawson

CASTING

Casting Director
Janine Snape
Artist Engagement Coordinator
Daphne Quah

PRODUCING

Senior Producer
Stephen Moore
Producer
Jess Burns
Company Manager
Julia Smith
Deputy Company Manager
Blaze Bryans

DEVELOPMENT

Director of Development
Rupert Sherwood
Annual Giving Manager
Meaghan Donaldson
Philanthropy Coordinator
Charlotte Menzies-King
Business Development Manager
José Ortiz
Business Development Coordinator
Jahnavi Shivakumar

EDUCATION & FAMILIES

Director of Education & Families
Jeremy Rice
Learning Manager
Nick Tranter
Education Content Producer
Emily Doyle
Education Coordinator
AD Chakraborty
Deadly Creatives Project Officer
Emma Holgate

PEOPLE & CULTURE

Director of People & Culture
Joanna Geysen
People & Culture Business Partner
Maddison Ryan
Receptionist
David Zierk

FINANCE & IT

Finance Manager
Andrew Slee
Assistant Accountant
Nicole Chong
IT & Systems Manager
Michael Schuettke
IT Support Officer
Darren Snowdon
Payroll Officer
Julia Godinho
Payments Officer
Jennifer Young
Building Services Manager
Adrian Aderhold

MARKETING & COMMUNICATIONS

Director of Marketing & Communications
Chris MacDonald
Head of Marketing
Claire La Greca
Marketing Campaign Manager
Aayushi Parikh
Program Marketing & Activation Lead
Rebecca Lawrence
Producer – Industry & Audience Initiatives
Laura Harris
Digital Engagement Manager
Jane Sutherland
Digital Coordinator
Harrison Buikstra
Lead Graphic Designer / Art Director
Kate Francis
Graphic Designer
Sarah Ridgway-Cross
Head of Communications
Isabella Ramdhanie
Communications Manager
Tilly Graovac
Publicity Consultant
Good Humans PR

PRODUCTION

Director of Technical & Production
Adam J Howe
Senior Production Manager
Michele Preshaw
Production Manager
Margaret Murray
Production Administrator
Alyson Brown
Production Coordinator
Zoe Rabb
Technical Manager – Electrics
Allan Hirons
Technical Coordinators – Electrics
Nic Wollan, Max Wilkie
Electrics Workshop Supervisor
Marcus Cook
Production Technician
Ounie Witherow Aitken
Production Technicians & Operators – Casual
Max Bowyer
Stella Dandolo
Claire Ferguson
Isaac Grubb
Sidney Millar
Gemma Rowe
Technical Manager – Staging & Design
Andrew Bellchambers
Production Design Coordinator
Jacob Battista
Props Coordinator
Jess Maguire
Head Mechanist
Tobias Chesworth

PROPERTIES

Properties Supervisor
Geoff McGregor
Props Maker
Colin Penn

SCENIC ART

Scenic Art Supervisor
Colin Harman
Scenic Artists
Alison Crawford
Colin Harman
Nellie Summerfield

WORKSHOP

Workshop Supervisor
Andrew Weavers
Deputy Workshop Supervisor
Simon Juliff
Set Makers
Sarah Hall
Nick Gray
Philip De Mulder
Peter Rosa
Welder
Ken Best

COSTUME

Costume Manager
Kate Seeley
Costume Cutters
Jocelyn Creed
Lyn Molloy
John Van Gastel
Costume Cutters – Casual
Emma Ikin
Costume Buyer
Carletta Childs
Millinery
Phillip Rhodes
Costume Hire
Liz Symons
Costume Maintenance – Casual
Jodi Hope
Claire Munnings

STAGE MANAGEMENT

Head of Stage Management
Whitney McNamara
Resident Stage Manager
Oriana Papa
Stage Managers – Casual
Morgan Clyne
Haydon Dickie
Zsuzsa Gaynor-Mihaly
Mercedes Gowlett
Juliette Hirons
Rain Iyahen
Annah Jacobs
Jess Keepence
Jenny Le
India Lively
Jessie McGuigan
Tom O'Sullivan
Lucie Sutherland
Pippa Wright

CRM & AUDIENCE INSIGHTS

Director of CRM & Audience Insights
Jerry Hodgins
Database Specialist
Ben Gu
Data Analyst
Sionna Maple

CUSTOMER EXPERIENCE & COMMERCIAL

Director of Customer Experience & Commercial
Brenna Sotiropoulos
Head of Customer Experience
Jessie Phillips
Ticketing Services Administrator
Hannah Flannery
VIP Ticketing Officer
Michael Bingham
Education Ticketing Officer
Mellita Ilich
Subscriptions & Telemarketing Team Leader
Peter Dowd
Events Manager
Mandy Jones
Southbank Theatre Operations Coordinator
Drew Thomson
Box Office Supervisor
Darcy Fleming
Box Office Duty Supervisors
Julie Leung
Jessica Pearson
Box Office Attendants
Stephanie Barham
Tanya Batt
Britt Ferry
Casey Gould
Min Kingham
Julia Landberg
Brigid Meredith
Michael Stratford Hutch
Lee Threadgold
Rhian Wilson
House Supervisors
George Abbott
Tanya Batt
Matt Bertram
Zak Brown
Kasey Gambling
Abby Hampton
House Attendants
Rhiannon Atkinson-Howatt
Stephanie Barham
Emily Busch
Briannah Borg
Zak Brown
Sam Diamond
Liz Drummond
Leila Gerges
Hugo Gutteridge
Abby Hampton
Michael Hart
Elise Jansen
Kathryn Joy
Natasha Milton
Ernesto Munoz
Brooke Painter
Lucy Pembroke
Brigid Quonoey
Taylor Reece
Solomon Rumble
Sophie Scott
Mieke Singh Dodd
Ayesha Tauseef
Olivia Walker
Rhian Wilson

SOUTHBANK THEATRE

Production Services Manager
Frank Stoffels
Lighting Supervisor
Geoff Adams-Walsh
Deputy Lighting Supervisor
Tom Roach
Sound Supervisor
Joy Weng
Deputy Sound Supervisor
Will Patterson
Fly Staging Supervisor
Adam Hanley
Deputy Fly Supervisor
Callum O'Connor
Stage & Technical Staff – Casual
Jon Bargen
Suzy Brooks
Connor Brown
Sam Bruechert
Jake Burger
Emily Campbell
Steve Campbell
Will Campbell
Bryan Chin
Harrison Cope
Gideon Cozens
Bryn Cullen
Kit Cunneen
Max Evans
Nick Eynaud
Mitch Forde
Mitchell Forden
Justin Gardam
Alex Giroud
Carla Grcic
Spencer Herd
Ethan Hunter
Marcus Macris
Alexandre Malta
Terry McKibbin
David Membery
David Murray
Sharna Murphy
Alix Otenstein
Jack Palmer
Marco Pezzimenti
Daniel Price
Jake Rogers
Jared Ross
Gemma Rowe
Taishah Simcox
Nathaniel Sy
Tom Vulcan
Dylan Wainwright-Berrell
Darcy Ward
James Williams
Nathaniel Zienow-Sy

OVERSEAS REPRESENTATIVE

New York
Kevin Emrick

Our Donors

We gratefully acknowledge the ongoing support of our leading Donors.

LIFETIME PATRONS

Acknowledging a lifetime of extraordinary support.

Rowland Ball OAM &
The Late Monica Maughan
Pat Burke
Peter Clemenger AO &
The Late Joan Clemenger AO
Greig Gailey &
Dr Geraldine Lazarus
Jane Hansen AO & Paul Little AO
Allan Myers AC KC &
Maria Myers AC
The Late Biddy Ponsford
The Late Dr Roger Riordan AM
Maureen Wheeler AO &
Tony Wheeler AO
The Late Ursula Whiteside
Caroline Young &
Derek Young AM

ENDOWMENT FUND DONORS

Supporting Melbourne Theatre Company's long-term sustainability and creative future.

Leading Gifts

Jane Hansen AO & Paul Little AO

$10,000+

Charles Gilles & Penny Allen

$5,000+

Prof Glyn Davis AC &
Prof Margaret Gardner AC

$1,000+

Judy Dunster

PLAYWRIGHTS GIVING CIRCLE

Supporting the NEXT STAGE Writers' Program, our industry-leading commissioning initiative.

Tony & Janine Burgess, Fitzpatrick Sykes Family Foundation, Jane Hansen AO & Paul Little AO, Larry Kamener & Petra Kamener, Susanna Mason, Prudence & Neil Morrison, Helen Nicolay, Pimlico Foundation, Tania Seary & Chris Lynch, Craig Semple, Dr Richard Simmie, Andrew Sisson AO & Tracey Sisson, Derek Young AM & Caroline Young

TRUSTS & FOUNDATIONS

The Gailey Lazarus Foundation

Annual giving

Acknowledging Donors whose recent gifts help enrich and transform lives through the magic of theatre.

Current as of January 2026.

BENEFACTORS CIRCLE

$50,000+

Krystyna Campbell-Pretty AM
Peter Clemenger AO
The Helen Fraser Giving Fund
Jane Hansen AO & Paul Little AO
Martin & Loreto Hosking
Craig Semple
Andrew Sisson AO & Tracey Sisson
Maureen Wheeler AO & Tony Wheeler AO

$20,000+

Tony & Janine Burgess
Fitzpatrick Sykes Family Foundation
Petra & Larry Kamener
Suzanne Kirkham
Prudence & Neil Morrison
Tania Seary & Chris Lynch
Orcadia Foundation LTD

$10,000+

Alan & Mary-Louise Archibald Foundation
John & Lorraine Bates
Jay Bethell & Peter Smart
Michael Buxton AM & Janet Buxton
Angie & Colin Carter
The Cattermole Family
Karen Cusack
Ann Cutts
Jennifer Darbyshire & David Walker
The Dowd Foundation
Christine Gilbertson
Charles Gillies & Penny Allen
Linda Herd
Daryl Kendrick & Leong Lai Peng (Betty)
Helen Lynch AM & Helen Bauer
Susanna Mason
McKellar Outram Foundation
Helen Nicolay
Pimlico Foundation
Catherine Quealy
The Reid Malley Foundation
Lisa Ring
Dr Richard Simmie
Rob Stewart & Lisa Dowd
Tintagel Bay P/L
Ralph Ward-Ambler AM & Barbara Ward-Ambler
Anonymous (2)

$5,000+

Joanna Baevski
Bagôt Gjergja Foundation
James Best & Doris Young
Deanne Bevan & Guy Russo
M & J Blythe
Bowness Family Foundation
Dr Douglas Brown & Treena Brown
Nan Brown
Dr Andrew Buchanan & Peter Darcy
Ian & Jillian Buchanan
Bill Burdett AM & Sandra Burdett
Pat Burke & Jan Nolan
Diana Burleigh
Alison & John Cameron
S Capp
S Crowe
Prof Glyn Davis AC & Prof Margaret Gardner AC
Andy Dinan & Mario Lo Giudice
Marian Evans
Patricia Faulkner AO
Diana & Murray Gerstman
Heather & Bob Glindemann OAM
Roger & Jan Goldsmith
Lesley Griffin
Jane Grover
David & Lilly Harris
Tony Hillery & Warwick Eddington
Bruce & Mary Humphries
Ian & Titania Henderson Foundation
Amy & Paul Jasper
Alex Lewenberg
Libby McMeekin
George & Rosa Morstyn
The Louise & Martyn Myer Foundation
Tom & Ruth O'Dea
Leigh O'Neill
OneTomorrow Charitable Fund
Dr Kia Pajouhesh (Smile Solutions)
Bruce Parncutt AO
A Penn & K Blauhorn
Planning Partners Pty Ltd
Renzella Foundation
Jeremy Ruskin & Roz Zalewski
Lynne Sherwood
Gordon & Faye Shinewell
Janet Whiting AM & Phil Lukies
SALT Catalyst
Price & Christine Williams
Anonymous (8)

ADVOCATES CIRCLE

$2,500+

Ian Baker & Cheryl Saunders
Jenny Barbour
Paul & Wendy Bonnici & Family
Jenny & Lucinda Brash
Bernadette Broberg
C Christian
Geoff Cosgriff
Susan Dahn
Ann Darby
Megan Davis
Kaye & John de Wijn
Pam Durrant
Melody & Jonathan Feder
Anna & John Field
Rosemary Forbes & Ian Hocking
Nigel & Cathy Garrard
The Mary Elinor Harris Fund Endowment
Lording Family Foundation
Colin & Helen Masters
Heather & Simon McKeon
Sandra Murdoch
Nelson Bros Funeral Services
Dr Paul Nisselle AM & Sue Nisselle
Roger & Ruth Parker
Christopher Reed
John & Veronica Rickard
Margaret Sahhar AM
Scanlon Foundation
Dr John Sime
Geoff Steinicke
James & Anne Syme
Frank Tisher OAM & Dr Miriam Tisher
Liz Tromans
The Ray & Margaret Wilson Foundation
Tony & Gillian Wood
Anonymous (3)

LOYALTY CIRCLE

$1,000+

E Abbott & B McComb
Prof Noel Alpins AM & Sylvia Alpins
Julie Andrews
Margaret Astbury
Prof Robin Batterham
Sandra Beanham
G J Bibby
Tara Bishop
Judy Bourke
Nigel & Sheena Broughton
Beth Brown & The Late Tom Bruce AM
Jannie Brown
Lynne & Rob Burgess
Julie Burke
Katie Burke
Geoffrey Bush-Coote & Michael Riordan
Pam Caldwell
John & Jan Campbell
Jessica Canning
F & M Carey
Clare Carlson
Chernov Family
Assoc Prof Lyn Clearihan & Dr Anthony Palmer
Judge Susan Cohen
Sandy & Yvonne Constantine
Deborah Conyngham
Jutta Cowen
Sue & John Denmead
Dr Sally Duguid & Dr David Tingay
J Dunster
Bev & Geoff Edwards
Karen & David Elias
Nita Eng
Anne Evans & Graham Evans AO
Dr Alastair Fearn
Peter Fearnside & Roxane Hislop
Paul & Mary Fildes
Grant Fisher & Helen Bird
Elizabeth Foster
Bruce Freeman
Kerry Gardner AM & Andrew Myer AM
Gaye & John Gaylard
Gill Family Foundation
Fiona Griffiths & Tony Osmond
Ian & Wendy Haines
M D Harper
Luke Heagerty
Gary & Susan Hearst
Lorraine Hendrata
Dr Alice Hill & Mark Nicholson
Brett & Kerri Hereward
Howard & Glennys Hocking
Emeritus Prof Andrea Hull AO
Nanette Hunter
T Johnson
Sally & Rod Johnstone
Lesley & Ian Jones
Michael Kantor
Benny Katz
Leah Kaplan & Barry Levy
Irene Kearsey & M J Ridley
Daniel Kilby
Fiona Kirwan-Hamilton & Brett Parkin
Doris & Steve Klein
Marianne & Arthur Klepfisz
Larry Kornhauser OAM & Natalya Gill
Jane Kunstler
S Lansbury & D Di Fabio
Glenda & Greg Lewin AM
Peter & Judy Loney
Lord Family
Kerryn Lowe & Raphael Arndt
K. Mackinnon
Natasha & Laurence Mandie
Chris Maple
Ian & Judi Marshman
Don & Sue Matthews
Paula McKinnon & Troy Sussman
Garry McLean
Emeritus Prof Peter McPhee AM
Fiona Menzies
Robert & Helena Mestrovic
John G Millard & Andrew Cason
MK Hope
Barbara & David Mushin
Sarah Nguyen
Nick Nichola & Ingrid Moyle
Dr Rosemary Nixon AM
In loving memory of Richard Park
Dr Annamarie Perlesz
Peter Philpott & Robert Ratcliffe
Nathan & Susan Pinskier
Victoria Ponsford
Phil & Gayle Raftery
David Reckenberg & Dale Bradbury
Sally Redlich
Victoria Redwood
Roslyn & Richard Rogers Family
S & S Rogerson
B & J Rollason
Nick & Rowena Rudge
Edwina Sahhar
Alex and Brady Scanlon Giving Fund
FE Scott
Sally & Tim Scott
Jacky & Rupert Sherwood
Diane Silk
Pauline & Tony Simioni
Jan Simon
Jane Simon & Peter Cox
Rachel Slade
Angela Smith

Annette Smorgon
Anthony Steward
Dr Ross & Helen Stillwell
Rosemary Stipanov
Shannon Super
Irene & John Sutton
David & Angela Taft
Rodney & Aviva Taft
Charles Tegner
The Veith Foundation
John & Anna van Weel
Kevin & Elizabeth Walsh
Pinky Watson
Ann & Alan Wilkinson
Robert & Diana Wilson
Mandy & Edward Yencken
Anonymous (25)

EDUCATION GIVING CIRCLE

Alan & Mary-Louise Archibald Foundation
Joanna Baevski
G J Bibby
Judy Bourke
Deborah Conyngham
Geoff Cosgriff
Ann Darby
Luke Heagerty
Larry Kornhauser OAM & Natalya Gill
Heather & Simon McKeon
Christopher Reed
John & Veronica Rickard
Roslyn & Richard Rogers Family
Scanlon Foundation
Gordon & Faye Shinewell
Jane Simon & Peter Cox
Rob Stewart & Lisa Dowd
Ann & Alan Wilkinson
The John & Myriam Wylie Foundation
Anonymous (4)

FIRST NATIONS GIVING CIRCLE

John & Lorraine Bates
Linda Herd
Michael Kantor
Daniel Kilby
Jane Kunstler
Nathan & Susan Pinskier
Christopher Reed
Craig Semple

Thank you

Melbourne Theatre Company would like to thank the following organisations for their generous support.

Major Partner

Future Directors Initiative Partner

MinterEllison.

Major Marketing Partner

The Monthly

The Saturday Paper

Season Partner

Supporting Forum Nights

TIME & PLACE Presents PARK MODERN

Associate Partners

Challis & Company Tomorrow's leaders today

Frontier software Human Capital Management & Payroll Software/Services

Intrepid

THE LANGHAM MELBOURNE

SCOTCHMANS HILL BELLARINE PENINSULA VICTORIA ESTABLISHED 1982

Supporting Partners

CARGO CREW

COMMUNE WINE

Genovese Coffee

invicium

THE LUXURY NETWORK

METROPOLIS EVENTS

QUEST SOUTHBANK

southgate

Wilson Parking

Marketing Partners

CINEMA NOVA

RRR

Southbank Theatre Partner

mgc THE MELBOURNE GIN COMPANY

Business Collective Members

Committee for Melbourne

Leadership Collective Australia

Schuler Shook

Current as of February 2026.